Broken Road
to Redemption

by Jamihla Young

You have purpose. Never
give up.

Much
Love,
JY

Jamihla Young was born and raised in Mansfield, Ohio by a single mother. In her debut book *Broken Road to Redemption* she gives readers insight on her life. Growing up broken and at times not understanding the world around her, she takes readers on a roller-coaster ride as she makes her journey from being a broken child to a woman finding redemption from her past. She reminds us that we are not our mistakes, we are not our circumstances and we are all worthy of being redeemed. Enjoy!

To my grandmother Joan Day
and my cousin/brother Nolan Lovett:
without you two I wouldn't be
the person I am today.

You are loved and truly missed.

ACKNOWLEDGEMENTS

Writing this book may have been one of the hardest things I've ever done in my life. So first and foremost, I would like to thank God for giving me the strength and the fortitude to complete it. I would like to thank my mother Stacey Young for putting up with all my shenanigans as I grew into the woman I've become today and for never giving up on me. I would like to thank my aunt Danielle Young for showing me that no matter what you go through, never give up on your dreams. To my little brothers Jermaine Hawthorne and Asante' Wilder, thank you for giving me a reason to want to be a better person. To my best friend Monique Hylton-Treasure, thank you for all your love and support and encouragement on my journey to becoming who I am now and for always being there no matter what. Sherri Jones thank you for all of your encouragement and support. Special thank you to Chai-Yehova for all the hours spent counseling and your encouragement. Thank you to Barbara Francis and Dr. Vonda for the time you spent editing my book; you are very much appreciated. Thank you, Tracey Hylton-Fuller, for your feedback and for the beautiful prayer at the end of this book. To Marsha Hylton, thank you for your awesome synopsis for this book. I would like to thank Angela Townsend and Georgann Turano-Hoose for being a part of my focus group. Special thank you to Ingrid Rizo for your help bringing my book cover to life. Thank you to my best friends Maria Black, Ishiera Brooks, and Tonnisha Lindsay for always riding with me through the good and the bad times. To Shaunqua, Shantia and Sharee Crawford and Mario Young, thank you for showing me that no matter what heartache this world throws at you, there is always a reason to keep pushing forward. Thank you to Pastor Melva Perry for prophesying back in 2016 that this book would one day be a reality. To my sisters Tiffany Williams, Shantrese Sykes, Cassandra Bowman, Ashley Howell and Alecia Howell thanks for always rooting for me. To my god children Trinitee, Treasure, and Rashad know that you are loved.

CONTENTS

FOREWORD

I met this unfiltered, brutally honest, no-nonsense, my way or the highway, self-assured, young lady over nine years ago. I witnessed her highs, lows, and in-betweens and watched in awe as Jamihla allowed God to transform her from the inside out. She is a living example that what the enemy means for evil, God can turn around for good.

Broken Road to Redemption details the sequential journey of Jamihla's life; it is an emotional rollercoaster. Our hearts will race as Jamihla shares thrilling experiences that evoke laughter, tears, and at times outrage. With each turn of the page, we will be empowered by Jamihla's transparency and encouraged to take a deeper look into the areas of our lives we avoid.

This memoir is a raw reminder that our lives are not our own and there are consequences to every decision we make. It is hope for those who feel beyond repair. *Broken Road to Redemption* is a testimony telling us we can never be so low or fragmented that God cannot reach us, dust us off, and put the pieces of our lives back together again.

I'm so proud of Jamihla's courage to share her story with the world and truly honored to call her my friend!

Monique Hylton-Treasure

PROLOGUE

This is my story! Some may not like it; many will feel uncomfortable while reading, but this is how things were seen through my eyes. Some things are still hard to talk about because of who I was. In retrospect, I cannot believe I was really that person.

My intent in telling my story is that hopefully someone reads it and it helps them. We are not our circumstances; we are not what people say we are. We all make mistakes; that is a part of life. We don't have to live in shame or guilt over our past. Everything we've done, everything we've been through, does not define us, but it does help mold us into the people we are today.

I would not be the person I am today if it weren't for the experiences I had in my life. I am not ashamed of my past. My life went the way it did because I saw myself, my surroundings, and people through my eyes. Only when I got the revelation of who I was through God's eyes did my life completely change. Well, enough of the chatter; stick with me, and you'll see what I mean.

CHAPTER 1

From as far back as I can remember, which is only to about 4th or 5th grade, I looked forward to two favorite things in the whole world: playing basketball and going to my grandma's house. I was good at basketball from the first time I picked one up. It was something that just came naturally; dribbling was one of my favorite things to do. When I was little, I could do things like dribble between my legs and behind my back, skills most little girls my age didn't possess. I would always find myself playing with boys a lot because there weren't many girls where I lived who played basketball.

That was one of the reasons I loved going over my grandma's house so much. There would always be someone at the park playing and I would get to see all my cousins and have a blast, from playing hide and seek and freeze tag to playing school, where we would actually take field trips to the park, with packed lunches and everything!

Those were the good old days, I tell you, before things became so complicated. My grandmother would always have our favorite snacks, every kind of cereal you could think of, every Disney movie, and she would cook almost every single night. There was no one who could cook better than my grandma, no one! For the most part I just loved being around her, cooking with her, going grocery shopping with her and watching TV shows like *Law and Order*.

I remember every time she would lie down to go to bed, she would have my cousins and me take turns rubbing her back. We would rub her back and she lay there and talk to us. So, we kind of appreciated this one-on-one time with her.

Looking back, I laugh because I realize she had her own free massage parlor. Still, all and all, I loved seeing my grandmother happy and that's what was most important. I don't know if it was because I was her first granddaughter or what, but we had a bond that was unbreakable.

CHAPTER 2

I was also blessed to know my great-grandmother. She lived right across the street from my grandma. We called her Gramma. My great-grandfather actually built both my grandmother's and great-grandmother's houses. He also built my Aunt Barbara's house; she lived next door to my grandma. I never got the chance to meet him.

If I was sick and my mom had to work, off to Gramma's house I went. She would make me soup and love on me and make me watch stories (afternoon soap operas) with her, which I hated but I never told her that. Often after school, my cousins and I would go to her house to wait for our parents to get off work. We would play games and pretend like we were on Showtime at the Apollo or act like some music group. We would take Kroger bags and jump off the front porch and act like they were parachutes. Sometimes she would load all of us up in the van and take us to the butcher shop with her. The butcher would always give us something random like a hotdog or piece of bologna.

My Gramma was one of the sweetest people you would ever meet, and she could bake her behind off. Nobody made peach cobbler like her. Even though she was sweet, if you cut up you were going to the backyard to her big tree to pick a switch off of it. And boy, oh boy, you didn't dare come back with something little because if she had to go get it, it was going to be 100 times worse. Believe me, once she got done tapping your legs with that switch you didn't cut up anymore.

Unless your childhood was absolutely horrible it's easy to

overlook the negative things that happened. As human beings we tend to mentally block out negative experiences as a sort of coping mechanism. Even though I had a lot of fun as a kid, there were also things that started chipping away at me at a young age.

As I mentioned earlier, I loved to play basketball and I often found myself playing with the boys. After a while I realized they no longer really looked at me as a girl, especially when I was picked first over boys to play on a team. They would say stuff like, "You want to be a boy?" Or that I was gay and my Cousin Nolan would always take up for me. I would say, "Whatever," or "No, I'm not" to their ignorant comments but I would find myself thinking that maybe it was my fault they were feeling that way. Was it because I wore basketball shorts and t-shirts, which were considered boy clothes?

Looking back now, it's silly to think about feeling guilty about how I dressed. What else was I supposed to wear playing basketball, a skirt? How was I supposed to be ready to play whenever and wherever I went? Why couldn't I just think they might just be jealous, or were just being stupid boys and move on? It was because I was a child and I thought as a child. These were the first set of stones that were thrown that started chipping away at me.

I found myself coming to the park earlier and earlier and playing by myself or sitting out when the guys played. When asked if I wanted to play, I would lie and say I didn't feel like it that day, even though I always felt like playing. I started holding myself back a little so I wouldn't be labeled what I was not. Don't ever do that; don't ever hold back on your gifts because of how somebody else feels about you. If I knew then what I know now, things would have been totally different. But I had to be that insecure child to be the person I am today.

I started playing basketball for the school in about the 4th grade and by the time I was in the 5th grade I started seeing how popular girls' basketball was becoming. I now had friends who were girls that I could play with. I started seeing that girls who were older than me were really good and all of a sudden, I didn't feel so alone. I no longer felt weird; I felt like being a girl and loving basketball was normal.

CHAPTER 3

Time marched on and the summer before I was getting ready to enter middle school something happened with one of my cousins—but before I get into that, let me rewind and go back. Before you can understand what I'm about to say, you have to understand where it stemmed from. My great-grandmother used to make us go to church with her: Sunday school, Sunday service, Vacation Bible School in the summer. You name it, we were there.

My great-grandmother was a longstanding member of Mount Calvary Baptist church. There were some things I liked in Sunday school, for example, the story of Noah's Ark and when we had to do Easter and Christmas speeches. I would always make sure I memorized every line and practiced until it was perfect. But over-all—and hear me clearly—I hated church, especially this church. I hated it.

Mount Calvary had what I like to call a group of old biddies, that is, old women who had been in church their whole life and never learned the love of Christ. They were just mean and judg-mental for no reason. Don't try to tighten up on me now; anybody who has ever stepped foot in a church knows an old biddy. Always trying to 'shhh' you when it's not you talking; you can't chew gum or eat any snacks while sitting through the four-hour service with-out them telling you to spit it out.

You have to wait to be escorted by one of the ancient ushers to use the restroom while they're hunched over like no one can see them holding one finger in the air with their white gloved hand. They would try to grab you by the arm if they wanted you in a different place than where you were. They gossiped about everybody; meanwhile, their kids and grandchildren were the unruliest kids outside of church. They made me absolutely hate church. If I wasn't at church with my great-grandmother, my mom would make us go to church. We visited a couple of different churches before she found a church home.

The older I got the more I started to notice church cliques among the adults and the kids. To me, church kids were just as bad as kids in the world, if not worse. These were the same kids that would act like they could do no wrong when you would see them in church with their parents. But at school you would see them in the lunchroom talking about everybody. They would be smoking and drinking and you would hear more about them being sexually active than anyone else.

I never felt like I fit into that world. One thing about me even as a young child is that I couldn't stand fake people and I felt like I was always surrounded by them when I went to church. Whenever I would spend the night at my friend Asia's house, her mom would always make us go to church. I don't know which one I hated more, hers or Mount Calvary.

We would have to get up extra early and get into our stockings and dresses or skirts, because that's what you had to wear at that kind of church. We would get all dressed up to go sit through a six-hour service where the collection plate was passed around like ten times. And even as a small child—I'm talking like fourth and fifth grade—I used to sit there and think that this was ridiculous. I felt like I sat there an entire day and I still didn't know who God was. What a mess! A little kid not knowing what the problem was but recognizing that there definitely was one—I hated church.

In my teenage years my friend's mom, who always was like a second mom, would make us go to church, especially on New Year's Eve. You couldn't hit the streets until you brought the New

Year in with a church service. I have to admit her church seemed different, probably because their entire family went to that church. And I can't say I experienced the same thing there as I experienced in the other churches I visited in the past. They seemed ok but my mind was made up that I hated church.

And as I grew and the older I got, I felt like church people proved me right every single time. When I became an adult and was out in the world partying all the time, I would see a lot of people that attended one of the biggest churches in Mansfield. You had to be dressed to impress at this church. You had to be on point every time you walked through the doors. The same people that would be holier than thou on Sunday were the very people you saw in the bar the night before.

I don't want anyone to take what I'm saying the wrong way. I'm not out to bash the church, but these are the things that chipped away at me and made me hate church. As a child, I never once experienced a move of God in any of those churches. All I learned from church was that God loved us if we were good and obedient, but if we were disobedient, we were going to hell, straight to hell. Do not pass, go; do not collect two hundred dollars, straight to the pit you go!

I learned nothing about God's forgiveness or God's grace, or how if we make mistakes to take it to God and repent of your sins and you would be forgiven. Nope, I learned to feel guilty and condemned if I messed up. So when I was about 10 years old something happened and I knew because of it I would spend eternity in hell. It wasn't a question in my little mind whether I was going or not; it was a fact. And out of all those years in church I never learned anything different and so the attack of the enemy began.

In the summertime while our parents would be at work we would go over to my grandmother's house. She would also be at work and we would be babysat by older cousins. We would have so much fun in the summer. I had a lot of cousins and we would play from sun up until it was time to go home.

One day we were playing hide and seek and one of my cousins and I walked in a room and heard weird noises coming from the closet. We opened the door and there were two of our older cousins having sex. We slammed the door shut and took off running out of the room down the stairs and outside.

I was so confused by what I just saw I jumped on my bike and rode off like nothing happened. I told myself I didn't see anything because I didn't want to see anything. I wished I could go back in time and not open that door. I wanted this picture out of my head.

When I returned to my grandmother's house later that day one of my cousins was waiting on me. I tried to avoid her but she called my name. "Jamihla!" she said. Ugh, I didn't want to talk about anything and I had a feeling I already knew what this was about. I parked my bike on its kickstand and walked over to her, and we sat down on the steps. She explained to me how it was normal to be curious and ok to try stuff and that I would understand later because I would do the same exact thing one day.

I was nine years old and I didn't understand and I didn't want to understand; as far as I was concerned, I didn't know what she was talking about. The summer went on as if nothing ever happened and I continued to have fun with my cousins. A year later one of my cousins and I were playing around at my grandmother's house late one night and just as if the words spoken the previous summer were a curse, it took root on us this night and we decided to try what we saw our older cousins doing. Yes, two little kids who were cousins were having sex, or what we thought was sex. I know at this point you're shocked and disgusted. It is hard even writing about it without being disgusted myself. And this is what I like to call the turning point. This was one of those moments when something happened and I knew my life would never be the same.

I was riddled with so much shame and guilt that I hated myself and I knew I was going to hell. I knew what the Bible said about people who sinned and, in my mind, I knew that we committed a big sin. The only thought I had was of me burning in hell and I was terrified, terrified of the flames and how bad it would burn. But most of all, I was terrified of how angry my mother would be when she found out that I did something that would send me to the bottomless pit.

Oh my gosh! I knew that I could not let my mom find out—or anyone, for that matter. I cried so much in the days to come and I tried not to act weird, because I knew if I did my mom would know something was wrong. I also knew that if she found out she would hate me. These were my thoughts as a ten-year-old child.

After a few days I made myself ok with the fact that I would spend eternity in hell. I didn't want to but I accepted responsibility for what I did and I knew I would have to pay for it with my soul. For a while I was numb inside. My guilt and shame led to me not caring about engaging in sexual activities. This led to me having sex with one of my cousin's older friends. I didn't really want to do it but he wanted to and I thought what difference would it make anyway? I felt so gross afterwards and even more guilt and shame, which I didn't even think was possible. So I told myself even though I was already going to burn I didn't want to make it any worse so I wasn't going to have sex again. And I didn't, not for a very long time.

After a while I was able to suppress the thoughts about what happened but every couple of months, I would hear this little voice that said, "Don't forget what you did and where you're going!" I would find myself scared, disgusted, and ashamed all over again. I would remember where my soul was destined and I would slip down into what I now know was depression.

CHAPTER 4

The new school year was rolling around and regardless of what happened that summer, I was excited. I would be attending John Simpson Middle School and I couldn't wait to go. Leaving elementary and going to middle school was a sign that one was getting older, and I was transitioning from a little kid to a big kid now.

My grandmother took me school shopping. We went out of town this year to shop. She bought me clothes none of the other kids here would have. I was still into skirts and this year tennis skirts were really popular. She bought me a black Nike tennis skirt with a white and black polo shirt to match and some black and white Nike tennis shoes. I got a bunch of other stuff but this was the outfit I couldn't wait to wear.

Everyone knows that feeling before the first day of school. You lay your clothes out and put your new book bag beside them, and you can barely sleep from anticipation of rocking all your new stuff the next day. I lived down the street from my new school and I could actually see it from my front porch. The things we get excited about as a kid. I would be able to walk to school this year, and this was also something I was excited about. I tried to go to bed early that night but I could barely sleep, tossing and turning until my alarm went off that next morning.

My mom checked on me that morning to see if I was nervous and to make sure I had everything. I was a little nervous but I had everything and I was ready to go. I grabbed my backpack checked myself in the mirror twice and I was out the door. I couldn't wait to see all my friends and meet all my new teachers. I was a dork in that way.

When I got to the front of the school there were kids everywhere; they were on the sidewalks and spread out across all the stairs that led up to the doors of the school. It was a sight to take in compared to what I was used to in elementary school.

The eighth graders looked so much older than us. This was starting to feel a little intimidating. I saw a group of my friends and they threw their hands up and motioned me to come over. I walked over and everybody was looking 'fly,' as to be expected. The bell rang and we were off to our first day of middle school.

It was everything I expected and more; it was bigger, I liked all my teachers so far and it seemed like we would be having fun in my classes this year. I especially couldn't wait for the mock trial that one of my teachers told us about. It sounded like fun.

I was told one of the counselors would be meeting with me later in the week to discuss the TAG (talented and gifted) program, which I was a member of while in elementary school.

The cafeteria food was better, the teachers were cooler, and I didn't have to ride the bus. I thought I would like my new school.

At the end of the day a group of us who were walking home together gathered in front of the school. Most of these kids were walking to the north side of town. I knew some of them from playing basketball and going to summer fun at Johns Park.

Everybody was walking and I was not that far from my house when one of the older boys who had been talking loudly the entire time yelled out, "Look at her fat ass knees!" He then looked at me and asked, "Why are your knees so big?" I heard laughter as I just shook my head, confused and horrified. I hung my head and heard this girl Candice, who was a grade ahead of me, telling him to shut up with his big dry ass lips.

Everyone began to laugh as she started 'roasting' him, and I was relieved the attention was off me. I appreciated her so much for that but the damage was already done. Whoever said words don't hurt was a liar and an idiot; words have the power to do more damage than any stone could ever do. In that split second, with his spoken words, another chip was gone out of me.

I know it sounds silly to those who don't understand the psyche of pre-teen or teenage girls. But the time frame between middle school and high school is when girls are starting to discover how they feel about themselves and sadly, what their peers think of them matters. So, in this one moment where a stupid boy who wasn't even cute said something about me, it made me hate a part of myself and the self-examination began.

I now hated wearing skirts and would only wear them when I absolutely had to. Once I started hating my knees, I noticed how my butt was bigger than most girls and I hated that too. Boys in school would make comments, not necessarily mean ones all the time, but the fact that anyone noticed it made me uncomfortable.

So I started wearing jeans and t-shirts that were a little too big so they would hang over my butt. Then I noticed how big my upper arms were, so I hated them too. I almost never liked wearing girl shirts or tank tops and when I played basketball, I always wore a t-shirt under my jersey.

Then the gap in my two front teeth started to bother me, so I went from being a kid who loved to smile to only really smiling when I was forced to. I started to hate everything about myself; the only thing I didn't hate was my hair.

I had always had long, pretty hair and that was one thing I always got compliments about. Even though I had so many internal struggles, I kept everything to myself because I didn't want to ever be seen as weak. I have been like that as far back as I can remember; I never wanted people to know things got to me.

I can't remember exactly when the color of my skin started

to bother me, but I never really thought about the difference in skin tones between my mother, my brothers and me until people started making comments. It was just something I never really thought about as a kid, but the older I got the more I noticed it. People would say stupid stuff like "you're acting light-skinned" or "you think you're better because you're light-skinned? What the heck! I'm not even light-skinned; I'm brown." My stepdad would say stuff like this to me all the time if he thought I had an attitude.

I started to feel like I didn't fit in and I didn't belong anywhere. There were many days I wished I looked like them, but I didn't and it began to bother me a lot. At one point I thought maybe I was adopted and they just didn't want to tell me. So, imagine hating the way you look and not looking like the people you see: 'chip, chip, chip.'

CHAPTER 5

In the year 1999, I was entering the eighth grade and this was exciting because this was the final year before I would be going to high school. I was excited until I found out we were moving and not only were we moving, we were moving to the south side of town.

I'm a north-sider all day long; the north side is where I was born and raised. Moving to the south side was a complete betrayal of my inner self. It may seem ridiculous to some but if you grew up in Mansfield, OH you knew how serious north-side, south-side rivalry was. It was stupid but it was also very real. People got into fights and people have even been shot because of what side of town they claimed they grew up on.

Not only was I leaving my side of town, I was leaving my school, Simpson, and being forced to go to our rival school, Malabar. I was not happy about this at all, but what could I do? I was only a kid and I had to do what I was told, and I was told I was moving and going to a new school. The first day of school I got up but the excitement that I had years prior was gone. I didn't want to go to a new school; I barely knew any of the kids who went there and worst of all I had to ride the bus again. Ugh! I hadn't ridden the bus since elementary. I know it had only been two years but it seemed like a lifetime ago.

We pulled up in the bus to the front of the building and I was in awe at how big this school was. Jeez! How was I ever going to find my way around here? There was a crowd of kids in front of the school. They were in different areas just like at Simpson; the only difference was that I really did not want to be here. But I put on a brave face and stepped off the bus.

As I began walking through the crowd, I saw people I went to elementary school with. I saw a couple of guys I knew were friends of my cousin Nolan. I heard my name and looked over and saw a group of girls across the walkway who I used to hang out with in elementary school.

I walked over and they were excited to see me. They couldn't believe I transferred schools that year. I told them that my family moved so I didn't really have a choice. A sense of relief flowed through me because now I didn't feel as alone and they could help me learn my way around. As soon as I exhaled in relief, I heard some commotion going on.

We turned around and saw this big light-skinned girl with a colored weave yelling and cussing at a smaller brown-skinned girl. A fight broke out and was quickly broken up by a couple of teachers. This school was viewed as the school of the suburbs! This was only the first day. I stood there, eyes wide, like, *What in the heck did I get myself into?*

As the school year went on, I made new friends and we became a tight-knit little group. I won't use people's actual names in the rest of the book because it is not my intent to tell their story, only my own. Basketball season was coming up and people were kind of hyped that I would be playing for Malabar this year.

I had played recreation ball the last three years and I'm not trying to toot my own horn, but I was rather good. I have so many trophies I don't even have space for all of them in my room. Basketball was my first love and the court was the only place I always felt like I belonged. Even though everything seemed ok outwardly I still had my secret struggles that no one knew about.

During this time, I wore looser jeans as opposed to fitted ones. The idea was to take attention away from my butt. I coupled that with wearing my hair in braids most of the time because it made it more manageable when I was playing basketball, and yep, you guessed it! The boys at my new school started rumors that I was gay. I wasn't gay; there were actually boys that I liked. "Why is me being gay always the go-to? Ugh!"

I would never let anyone see that it bothered me. I never went home and cried to my mom, and I never whined to my friends about it. If one of them brought it up I would just shrug it off and say whoever said that was dumb. I kept it locked away inside, like everything else. And just like clockwork that little voice popped up in the back of my head, telling me don't forget what you did or where you're going.

I still never told anyone about what happened; I couldn't. It was disgusting and too embarrassing. And even though I had a close group of friends at this point, they had so many problems of their own I couldn't imagine bringing mine up. I felt like I was always talking one of them off the ledge.

One of them suffered from depression and would cut her wrists at night when no one was around. She never cut deep enough to do real damage but she always cut enough to leave a scar. I didn't understand how no one else ever noticed. Another one was hands down the prettiest girl in school but battled anorexia, and the last one actually struggled with her sexuality but no one else knew. And these were all the secrets I had to keep on top of trying to keep myself on the right side of sanity. My friends were dysfunctional and clearly had problems, but I loved them and that was all that mattered.

CHAPTER 6

Eighth grade came to an end and we couldn't wait for summer to end. We would be in high school next year. Cheerleading tryouts were that summer and our friend Bianca had made the team. Her team was in a competition at the mall so my friend Aubrey and I went to support and show love. It was a while before Bianca and her team would be performing so Aubrey and I decided to go to the music store and look at CDs.

On our way in the store one of the older cheerleaders stopped us and asked if she could talk to me for a second. I knew her from around the park by my grandmother's house. I would go there and play basketball sometimes, especially in the summer. I said, "Sure" and told Aubrey to go ahead and that I would catch up with her in a minute.

As soon as Aubrey walked away the first thing the cheerleader asked was, "Hey, is that your girlfriend?"

I was thinking *what the heck* as I started nervously laughing like an idiot. "No, what would make you think that?" I replied.

She shrugged and said, "Nothing" and quickly changed the subject. She started asking me random questions. "How is your summer going?" "Are you ready for high school?"—stuff like that. I answered her questions and after a few minutes of chatting I told her that I had to catch up with my friend and that I would 'holla' at her later. As I was walking away, I was thinking that I hadn't even made it to high school yet and the juniors already thought I was gay Great!

The summer was pretty much a blur. It felt like it ended as

soon as it started. Freshman year started and I was officially in high school. I loved the fact that as freshmen we had our own building, so it was a little less intimidating.

The previous summer I started dating one of my cousin Nolan's friends who I had known for years. Growing up he would always come visit in the summer but now he would be here permanently since he relocated here from Dayton. We liked the same music and movies, we both loved basketball and whenever we were together, we always laughed nonstop. We really thought one day we would end up like Sanaa Lathan and Omar Epps in *Love & Basketball*.

School wasn't bad; the cafeteria food was much better than the cafeteria food in middle school, especially the French fries. My classes were ok and all the teachers seemed cool for now. I would be trying out for the freshman basketball team this year. I heard the coaches were pretty tough and that tryouts and practices could be brutal, but I was up for the challenge.

On the first day of conditioning I realized how true the statements about tryouts were. There were girls throwing up, I thought my legs were going to fall off, and girls were dropping like flies just because they couldn't take any more running. But my persistence paid off and I made the team and so did a few of my friends. We were so excited.

On the first day of practice we were running drills and the coach of the junior varsity team showed up. We figured she just popped in to see how things were going. She asked our coach if she could speak with him and they talked for a little while by the bleachers. When our coach walked back over to us, he told me to grab my stuff and follow the coach of the junior varsity team.

I was confused. I hadn't done anything wrong in school. I knew my grades were up to par. Oh shoot, maybe they said I made the team by mistake. I was a bundle of nerves and felt like I was going to throw up as I walked over to her. The JV coach looked at me and smiled as I asked what was going on. She said, "You're playing JV this year, not freshman! Let's go." I grabbed my orange and white Adidas duffle bag and followed her, feeling excited and torn at the same time.

The day I walked out of that gym things were never the same between the friends I made the team with and me. I would go to school in the freshman building and have to be taken to the main campus a few miles away for practice. I quickly made friends on my new team and some of the girls would start to pick me up from school to drive me to practice. This made some of my old friends feel some type of way and I was told I was acting funny now. I was even called a traitor once by one of my former teammates. That didn't even make sense in my mind; girls could be weird and so extra sometimes.

By the end of freshman year, I had gained many new friends who were all older than me. But my old friends and I started to drift apart. My boyfriend and I talked a little less. We had different schedules and he was playing basketball too. We never had time to hang out anymore and as a result we ended up taking a break; so much for *Love & Basketball*.

The school year finally came to an end and summer kicked in full swing with summer leagues and different basketball tournaments. I really didn't have much time for anything else and I can't really say I wanted to do anything else. With so much going on, the summer flew by and sophomore year was upon us. I had a few friends my age but most of my friends were seniors this year.

I started dating James, who was a year ahead of me in school. I was his moon and his stars and he was mine. He called me 'button' because he said I had a cute little button nose and I called him Hector Macho Camacho at his request! He was silly like that and still to this day one of the funniest people I have ever met. He would come to all of my games and whenever I had free time you wouldn't see me without him. If we weren't together, we would be talking on the phone.

A lot of the friends of the girl he used to date didn't like me so they kept throwing fuel on the rumor that I was gay. He didn't care about the rumor though, and he dared any of them to come near me. He didn't care about fighting and everybody knew it. Regardless of me having a boyfriend, every day I would still hear rumors about which girl I was supposed to be messing with now. Even though this had been the theme for a few years now, it still bothered me and every time I heard a new rumor that little voice would pop back in my head and say, "Don't forget what you did and where you're going." And regardless of how sweet and funny James was, he could never take my mind off that fact.

CHAPTER 7

At this point in high school I started to slip into a depression. I'd grown tired of the rumors and I was exhausted from always pretending that I was ok. I really didn't care that much about my grades; I just always made sure they were high enough to play basketball and keep my mom off my back. The rumors had gotten so bad that a few of my friends' parents became concerned and one in particular didn't want their daughter hanging around me anymore for fear that she would become a lesbian. This infuriated me, because this particular friend was already experimenting with other girls, not me. She just didn't fit the stereotype of what people think lesbians look like. And with this a slow rage started to boil deep down inside me and as that fire kindled, I started to hear that voice again: "Don't forget what you did and where you're going."

My attitude started to change a little and I became a little more withdrawn at home and I would rather be out in the streets with my friends. My temper was becoming out of control and if you said anything to me you better be ready to get a piece of my mind. And what could add more fuel to a fire already burning inside an insecure broken teenage girl? Alcohol! I loved the way it burned going down and it either numbed or amplified whatever I was feeling. I started off with stuff like Mike's hard lemonade and wine coolers. Drinking was nothing new to me; one of my friend's parents had been giving us alcohol since the eighth grade. They just made me swear I would never tell my parents. I would only drink on the weekends and sometimes would pay for it come Saturday morning practice. My drinking wasn't that bad yet, but like every seed that's planted, give it time and watch it grow.

I had a best friend on the basketball team, Amanda, who would graduate this year. Since I started on the team, we pretty much sat beside each other to and from every game. She would sometimes braid my hair for me before games. She carried a 4.0 GPA with honors, was a scholar athlete, could dance and was pretty. She was everything I wanted in a big sister and she never knew how much I looked up to her.

When I was with her and our other friends who were also seniors, they almost treated me as if I was a kid. They wouldn't let me drink and would always make sure I was home by 1:00 AM. It was almost comical how they thought they were protecting me from something. Little did they know what I didn't do with them I did with my other friends.

Of course, eventually rumors about Amanda and me started and it made me not want to be around her as much. Not so much for me, but I didn't want people thinking that about her. I felt like I had this huge sign on my back all the time that read 'Gay, gay, gay!' Anybody I would get close to, I either liked them or I was messing with them. Ugh! Why couldn't I just be Jamihla? Why wasn't that good enough? Why was someone always trying to label me? Chip, chip, chip.

Pretty soon people on the basketball team would start saying stuff too. I tried to have a conversation with an adult I was close to about how it was making me feel. Their response was, "If you are gay it's ok."

I replied, "I'm not, that's the problem. If I was it wouldn't bother me."

They replied, "The people saying those things are just stupid teenagers. Ignore them but if it's true, shoot, I'll watch." They started laughing and said they were just kidding.

I thought, *What in the hell? What kind of sick crap is that!* I had been ignoring people for years and it had only gotten worse. Ugh, I wished I had never said anything to them. Not only did they not give me advice, they sort of freaked me out. The only thing I took away from that conversation was I wasn't talking to any other adults about it.

Before basketball games and practices, I would go into where our old showers were in the locker room. No one ever used them to shower; there was rust in a lot of them and there was very little light back there. I would go back there and change so no one would feel uncomfortable. I was really starting to hate people. The only thing that actually brought me any joy or peace was my baby brother. He was about five then, and he thought the world of me and went everywhere I went. Football games, basketball games—you name it, he was right beside me.

It had been like that ever since he came home from the hospital. He even slept in my room every night and when my mom and my stepdad tried to break him from it, he would wait until they fell asleep. He would softly knock on my door and say, "Me-Me, is it ok to come in now?" That was my little guy, my shadow, and my biggest fan. He even had his own Tygers basketball jersey and when I would lead my team out of the tunnel for our games, he would be in front of the line leading me through the smoke. The coaches and the team loved him, and I loved this kid! Whenever I had a bad day, looking into his little eyes would make everything disappear.

CHAPTER 8

The cheerleader I mentioned earlier (Dominque) who had stopped me at the mall had become somewhat of a friend. We would talk on the phone and I even kept some of my books in her locker because it was close to my first period class. I really didn't think much of it; the locker was in a convenient location and she told me to feel free to use it. There were rumors that she was gay but at this point I didn't care; I didn't judge anybody. Look at all the lies people told about me that weren't true!

As the year went on James and I became closer and closer. The way I felt for him couldn't be measured by words. Everything was going great and then life smacked me in the face so hard I couldn't see straight. One of my family members on my father's side informed me that James and I were cousins. Yep, you heard it right—COUSINS! What in the hell was the deal with this cousin thing? Was I cursed? Why God, why is this happening? Neither of us had any idea that this could even be a possibility.

The only thing I knew about my father was his name and that he left when I was four. I met my two older sisters by him not too long ago but I didn't know much about them either. Nobody on my mom's side talked about him. And the first time I did ask my grandmother about him, she said "If I ever see him, I'm going to beat him with a hammer!" And that was the end of that inquiry.

I was heartbroken and James had an even harder time letting go. He didn't care what people said. It wasn't our fault; we didn't know. But I knew it was wrong and it had to end. And with that another huge chunk was gone—chip, chip, chip—and again the voice was back: "Don't forget what you did and where you're going." I felt like my life was on a downward spiral.

I was haunted by what happened when I was little, I recently found out I was dating my cousin and just about every day I heard a new rumor about me and what girl I was supposedly messing with. Screw this life; I didn't know how much more of this I could take. I shut my locker and headed to class.

I got to the elevators that were right by the principal's office in front of the main entrance. A fight broke out in the hallway a, huge crowd formed and I saw two girls, one I knew from passing in the halls and the other one lived around the corner from my house. A few punches were thrown and hair was flying before teachers came and broke it up and started yelling for people to return to class. The two girls were still yelling and cussing, trying to get back at each other while they were being pulled toward opposite ends of the hallway. The one who lived around the corner from me was being pulled past me.

As I was standing on the wall, she pointed directly at me and yelled, "B***h, you're next!" What? What in the hell did I ever do to her? I didn't even know she wanted to fight me. Whatever! Either way, that was it! I was sick of people. I'd had it. I dropped my books and took off full speed in her direction as she was trying to get to me and right as I got to her and cocked my arm back to throat punch her, I felt myself in the air. I was no longer on my feet. My principal had me hemmed up on the elevator doors, telling me to calm down. I was so angry I was seeing red and nothing was registering as I kicked and pulled to get out of his grasp.

The next thing I knew I was sitting in the principal's office as they tried to get a hold of my mother. I was sent home for the day and I had Wednesday afterschool detention and the other girl was suspended. I don't know why I had Wednesday detention; she was the one who started it, but whatever. After I explained to my mom what happened I was not in trouble at home but I was still pissed off.

A few weeks later I made it to the gym early before basketball practice, and the cheerleaders were finished and leaving the gym as I walked down the stairs to our locker room. I thanked God I would not have to change in the shower. I made it to the bottom of the stairs and through the doorway when I saw Dominique gathering up her stuff. She must have been the last one to get dressed. She said, "Hey, what's up?"

I replied, "Nothing, I had to stay after school for something so I came straight to the gym after to get ready for practice." I asked how their practice was and she said that it was all right. After small talk for a minute she began to walk out but walked over to me first and gave me a hug, which was not unusual, but then she pulled back a little and looked at me and then, boom! her lips were on mine. So many thoughts started running through my mind. *What is happening, do I like this, what in the hell is happening? Does this mean I'm gay? I'm not gay; what is happening?* And just as quickly as it began, it was over. She said something to me and I saw her lips moving but my mind wasn't working right then. She smiled and disappeared up the stairs.

A few seconds later a couple of my teammates walked in. Great! To the showers I went. As I was walking toward the showers, I thought about what just happened—as if my life wasn't complicated enough. In the days that followed I was still confused by what happened and in the many times we talked after, the subject was never brought up. I wanted to know why she did it but my mind couldn't formulate the words to ask her.

I finally decided I would talk to Aubrey about it. I was supposed to be staying at her house for the weekend. Once Aubrey and I were at her house chilling in the living room, I told her about what happened. I told her that I didn't know what to think about it. She asked how I felt and I told her I had no clue how I felt. It was all really confusing.

As our conversation went on Aubrey said she had something to tell me, so I told her to spill it. And she did; she spilled it all. I found out that one of our friends had been in a relationship with Dominique the prior year. I knew nothing about it! This made things even more weird. I still didn't know how I felt and on top of that, she used to date my friend. I was a ball of emotions and confusion so I thought it best to just tuck this in the back of my mind with all the other bad things. Dominique and I remained friends and nothing was ever spoken of that day in the locker room, but the seed was planted and another piece of the person I used to be was chipped away.

Sophomore year came to a close and a lot of my friends graduated that year; there were plenty of graduation parties, and graduation parties meant plenty of alcohol. I know what you're thinking—no, they didn't serve alcohol at the graduation parties but almost any teenager could get their hands on a bottle of liquor or beer at graduation parties. Amanda and my older friends would always try to keep me from drinking but they didn't stop anything. I would be at a party with them and still get drinks without them knowing.

That summer I realized how much I loved shots—shots of vodka, to be exact. And if I wasn't playing basketball or working my summer job that's what I was doing: drinking or getting high. Smoking always seemed to mellow me out when I wanted to just chill, and drinking would turn me all the way up when I really wanted to party. What I did was dependent upon what mood I was in that day. When I was high, I didn't have a care in the world; everything was funny and all the voices in my head that told me where I was going and that would point out all of my flaws would just fade away.

On the other hand, when I was drunk the voices would be pushed back but it didn't make me forget. In fact, it would make me angry and if you crossed my path the wrong way it could be a really bad night.

CHAPTER 9

Nobody knew about the internal struggles I was fighting every single day. I knew my mom could tell I was different but she didn't know why. Every so often she would ask if I was ok and if anyone had been messing with me or touching me. I would always reply with a quick "No, and why do you keep asking me that?" Part of me wanted to tell my mom everything; maybe she could have fixed it or maybe she could have fixed me and I wouldn't have felt so bad, so broken anymore. But the other part of me was terrified of what she would do if she found out. And that was right where the enemy wanted me.

Either way that kid who wanted help from my mom died some years ago. Now all that was left was the shell of a person riddled with holes from all the pieces that had been chipped away. And no one would ever know because I was so good at pretending. I was so good at acting like nothing bothered me and so good at giving my friends advice that no one would ever suspect a thing.

The bell rang and junior year began. Amanda was off at college that year so things felt a little different. But our friendship wasn't really the same after the summer. She met this dude and they started dating. At first, he was cool but after a while I could tell he didn't like me or didn't like me being around Amanda, especially when he heard the rumors that I was gay. The vibes were always weird so I just kind of fell back because I knew she really liked him. And I just wanted her to be happy.

During the summer Amanda's little sister Janiyah and I became really cool and started hanging out. She was a sophomore but almost everybody in their class was older than me because I started elementary school when I was four years old.

As junior year got underway, I was already over school. The boys were obnoxious and dumb. My other group of friends were still dealing with the same problems from when we were in eighth grade. There was always some drama about a boy. Somebody was talking to a boy the other one liked, or somebody was dating somebody's ex. It was so annoying and I was over teenage drama, period.

I would sit in class and hear the teachers talk but I wasn't listening. All I could think about was when class was going to be over. Everything about this life was annoying at this point. I didn't care about school; I didn't even care about basketball anymore.

The basketball season rolled around and tryouts were underway and that year I decided I no longer wanted to play. Teachers would ask me why; the coaches would ask me why and I would tell them all the same thing: "Because I don't want to!" What couldn't people understand? My coach never let up and after many conversations, with only two weeks left in tryouts, I finally agreed to go back.

I made the team and just as I was kind of getting back in the swing of things, report cards come out. My GPA had dropped to a 1.3 and I was deemed ineligible to participate in sports. My mother was furious, which I knew she would be; my coach was upset and crying. My mom asked, "How could you let this happen and why?" And I was sad they were upset and disappointed. But I didn't care; I didn't want to play anyway. I was just pissed I wasted my time.

I hated school and didn't want to be there; the only thing stopping me from thinking about ending it was I didn't want to go to hell any faster than I was already going. As to be expected, I was grounded for life or until I got my grades up, whichever came first. I didn't care; when I had to be at home, I just locked myself away in my room and read my books. I barely spoke to anybody in my house except my baby brother. He was still the only person that actually made me happy. Even my grandmother tried talking to me but it was too late. I felt like I had already checked out of that place. And just like clockwork that dumb voice entered: "Don't forget what you did and where you're going" As if I could ever forget! I already felt like I had one foot in hell anyway.

My mom thought maybe Amanda could talk some sense into me so she let me talk to her even though I wasn't allowed on the phone. Amanda was so mad and disappointed when she found out about my grades and of course, just like everybody else she asked what was going on, and what happened to me. And she got the same answer as everybody else. "I don't know, it is what it is, and there's nothing I can do about it now." When would these people realize they couldn't save me!

I finally got my grades up so I could get off punishment. My mom made me call home to check in more when I was out. She and my basketball coach thought it would be a good idea if I still traveled with the basketball team and helped keep stats, etc., I guess as an attempt to keep me busy and out of trouble. It wasn't terrible but I got tired of people saying how they wished I was out there and asking me what happened that year, why wasn't I playing? People can be so annoying!

The rest of my junior year was a blur; here one minute and then it was over! Thank God! That summer was a busy one, preparing for senior year. I had three different groups of friends that I alternated hanging out with. I also started playing basketball again at the behest of my family, and I had summer league. Summer league was always fun and we always dominated. With summer being so busy it flew by and I have to say I was starting to feel kind of good again, like I could see the light at the end of the tunnel of darkness.

I was chilling at home and my cell phone rang. It was a private number; I answered by saying, "Hello?" The girl on the other end started talking and said that she was from the church of Jesus Christ with this long name attached to it. She told me how it was wrong to be gay and asked who was I having sex with, Bianca or Aubrey. *What in the hell?* I thought. She started giggling and told me that I was going to burn in hell for being gay, and she continued rambling until I hung up

I was kind of in shock the first time so I didn't say anything, but I knew exactly who it was. It was this dumb girl in my class, Shannon, who was terrible at disguising her voice. She always did it when she and another girl from our class were at each other's house. The funny thing was I could have beat both of them up if I had really wanted to. They had no idea I knew it was them. But it was like what was the point in even confronting them, even though they were wrong about the reason. They weren't wrong about the fact that I was going to hell, and maybe this was another way for me to never forget it.

CHAPTER 10

Senior year started and I was excited—finally, my last year of high school. I would be graduating and I would be done with all these dumb kids. On the first day of school our administration called an assembly in the auditorium for the class of 2004. As we filed into the auditorium our principal was standing on the stage. The assembly was about what they wouldn't tolerate from us that year; I guess at this point we were the worst class to grace these halls. Who knew! I couldn't believe that we were actually sitting in a room being told how to behave?

And just when I thought administration had to be wrong about our class, people started booing the principal and throwing the papers that they gave us when we walked in at the stage. If this was any indication of how the year was going to be, I actually felt sorry for those teachers. I only had a few actual core classes; the rest were study halls and bull crap electives that I didn't actually need.

School had just started and I already couldn't wait for it to be over. Nothing really changed with my friends; they were all still doing the same stuff. Except they were messing with older guys now and yet still having the same drama. It was amazing that I could still be a topic of conversation, but I was, and it had taken me all those years not to give a damn about what any of those losers thought.

I was still drinking on the weekends but I smoked weed more than anything else. Sometimes I got high after school and it wore off just before my mom reached home. I made sure to keep my grades up; I didn't want a repeat of '03.

People seemed extra annoying that year. Everybody felt the need to check in with me to see how my grades were and if I was excited as we were approaching basketball season. I put on my best fake happy face and told people, "Yep," and I thought we were actually going to have a good team that year just to satisfy them so they would stop talking to me.

Basketball season kicked-off and before our first game some of the guys from the soccer team threw a party in the woods and a bunch of us from the team were invited. The idea of a party in the woods sounded kind of weird at first but then I was like what the heck, why not?

A couple of my friends and I decided to go. It was all the way out in Bellville, which was twenty minutes away, but the ride seemed like it was taking us an eternity. The farther we drove the more skeptical I was getting, and I started to think this was beginning to feel like the opening scenes of a scary movie. We drove down into a wooded area and we saw a bunch of cars parked but no people.

We parked and started to walk down this path that took us down a hill and once we walked for what seemed like a mile, we could see faint sparks of light at the bottom of the hill. We walked a little more and realized it was a bonfire. Man, I'd never had to exercise that much just to make it to a party.

When we finally got there, we saw that they had kegs set up in different locations, a bunch of coolers filled with ice, beer, and wine coolers. There were a bunch of chairs around the bonfire and a trailer off to the side that had smoke billowing out of it. Where in the hell did, they get a trailer from? You could see kids smoking and taking shots in there and God knows what else!

Someone tried to hand me a joint and I was like, "Naw, I'm good." I was not smoking anything I didn't see rolled. No offense but some of those white kids were wild. You didn't know what was in their stuff. I grabbed a beer and decided to take it easy I was out of my element out here. I didn't really know where I was and Mansfield was a good 20-30 minutes away. I needed to be aware of my surroundings at all times. I was not going out like the black chick in the beginning of the *Scream* movie.

We were having fun and some people were really wasted but nobody was acting up. I saw a group of kids coming down the hill the same way we came, and all of them had flashlights. They seemed a little over-prepared, even though having a flashlight would have been a good idea. One of them yelled out "Woo hoo, party!!!" There were like ten of them and they were getting closer. Wait a minute, kids don't walk like that. There was only one group of people that walked like that. One of them yelled, "Don't run and you won't be in trouble!" It was the POLICE!

Everybody looked up and you know what happened next: Everybody took off running except for one of my teammates, who was passed out on the picnic table. I was flying through trees and could barely see and this tall female cop with short blonde hair was after me. I was dipping and dodging through trees, "Dang it, man, why is this all uphill?" I finally put a little distance between me and her and then WHAM!! I ran smack dead into a tree. I was dazed for a few seconds and I rolled over just in time to see her run the wrong way. I got my bearings, and ran until I saw some light.

I saw one of my classmates in her car and she yelled, "Get in." I jumped in the backseat of her car; there were already three other people in the car, and she peeled out. Once we were in the clear we all started cracking up laughing. Man, that was close! She dropped me off at my house and I was forever grateful!! Good, my mom wasn't home yet. I took a bath and lay on my bed and thought, *Thank God, we got away!!*

On Monday when we went back to school, we heard about

who got caught and was taken home by the police; I was just thankful it wasn't me. I found out that my teammate who was passed out on the table was snoring through all the commotion and that the cops were true to their word. She didn't get in trouble because she didn't run. Let's be honest, though; she couldn't have run if she wanted too.

Basketball season was off to a good start. My GPA was still up. My mom wasn't on my back as much but I knew she didn't fully trust that the streak would last. A few weeks passed and Janiyah asked if I wanted to stay at her house and I said, "Sure." My mom talked to her mom and was cool with it. At the last-minute Janiyah said, "Let's stay at my sister Alexis' house" and I said, "Cool." So, we went to the boys' basketball game that night and after that I needed to get clothes from my house.

I was driving Janiyah's mom's car because her older sister allowed us to use it, even though none of us had licenses. I parked a little way up the street from my house right before you got to my neighbor's driveway so my mom couldn't see me driving. What an idiot! This plan was stupid from the beginning. I don't know if I really thought I was going to get away with it or I just didn't care. I ran into the house to grab my stuff and my mom was sitting on the couch in the living room. She asked what we were getting ready to do and I told her, "We are getting ready to go to Janiyah's house." That was a lie. We were going over her older sister Alexis' house. She said okay and I grabbed my stuff and left. She must have had x-ray vision because it was dark outside. I made sure not to park by the street light and we were all dressed the same.

We got to Alexis' house and we already had somebody who got us some liquor. We invited a couple of people over who Alexis knew nothing about. We always did this to her; she would cuss us out and then she would be over it. It was kind of like our little routine now.

A small get-together turned into a full-blown party and about an hour later my mom called. I stepped outside to answer my cell phone. "Hello?"

She said, "Where are you, and don't lie; I know you're not at Janiyah's." My heart sank! Ugh!

"I'm at Alexis'," I replied.

"Is that where you're supposed to be?" she asked "And furthermore, why in the hell were you driving? And don't say you weren't because I saw you."

I didn't even feel like going back and forth with her, so I just asked, "Do you want me to come home?"

She asked, "Do you want your ass whooped now or later? It's up to you." And she hung up.

I walked back in the house, put my phone in my pocket and grabbed a shot; no sense in ruining my night. "Bottoms up!" I decided I would take it later; I didn't go home that night. I got wasted because I knew she was going to kill me and I might as well enjoy my last night on earth.

I got back home around noon the next day with full expectations of her trying to kill me, but I didn't care. I walked in the house and she was not there. Classic parental psychological warfare; they know the waiting is the worst part. Well played, Mother, well played.

I sat in my room as hours passed, thinking, *Ugh, would she just hurry up already?* The time was going by so slowly, and six hours later I heard her car pull in the driveway; shortly afterward I heard the door shut as she walked into the house. As I was listening, I could hear her walk past my room and into her room, which was directly across the hall. Minutes ticked by slowly and my door burst open.

She walked in with a belt wrapped around her hand with the buckle part out. She started yelling at me, "SO YOU THINK

YOU'RE GROWN NOW?" She cocked back and I'm thinking, *she has completely lost it because she is trying to whoop me with a metal buckle.* She cocked back to swing and as her arm came down, I grabbed the belt. I don't know if the look on her face was horror or shock but I'm sure my face looked the exact same way, because I was just as shocked at my reaction as she was. And at that moment I went from not caring to full-on rebellion.

She tried to hit me again; this time I grabbed her wrist and I cannot even describe the look in her eyes. I'd never seen her this mad. I was not trying to hurt her; I was just trying to stop her from hurting me. My stepdad must have heard all the commotion because he ran into the room and pulled her away from me and tried to calm her down. I slammed my door and lay on top of my bed, and I knew there was no coming back from this.

It was quite some time before my mom spoke to me again and when she finally did it was to inform me that I was grounded until... She could have saved her breath because I already figured as much. But I just said, "Ok."

CHAPTER 11

I was only allowed to go to school, practice, and my games. I was already used to this routine; I seemed to find myself on punishment a lot.

A month went by and I was sitting in the gym at school because we had a home game later that evening so there was no sense in me going all the way home. A couple of girls I was cool with asked if I wanted to take a ride and smoke a blunt. Since I had almost three hours before my game, I said, "Why not?"

We piled in the car and hit a few corners before we found somewhere to park. There were four of us: me, the two girls who asked if I wanted to smoke and my PNC (partner in crime), who was also on the basketball team. One blunt would wear off way before the game so we were good. We decided to hotbox it. For those of you who don't know what that is, it means you smoke with all the windows up so the smoke can't escape and in turn you get a little higher. So, we were smoking and talking and laughing and before you knew it, one blunt turned into two blunts and the time flew by.

It was time for us to get back to the school. We pulled up to the front of the building. We got out and just stood there for a minute. We were as high as kites and we couldn't stop laughing. I tapped my PNC and said, "Come on, man, we have to pull our crap together." Before we walked into the building, we used one of the girl's body sprays but that did absolutely nothing to cover up the fact that we just sat in the car with the windows rolled up and smoked two blunts.

As soon as we walked up the stairs and into the gym people were trying to talk to us, but we went straight downstairs to the locker room and changed to get out of the weed-drenched clothes. When we finally went back upstairs to the gym area we sat in a section of the bleachers where no one was sitting and waited for the JV game to start. After a few minutes other teammates came and sat by us. Some were asking questions like, "What's up with you two?"

We just kept looking straight ahead and replied, "Nothing." One of them asked if we were high and I responded "No, why is everybody giving us the third degree? Y'all work for the police now?" It was so hard not to laugh.

The third quarter of the JV game came and all of us on the varsity team filed downstairs to the locker room to get ready for our game. The coach was talking to us and going over our game plan when I looked over and my PNC's eyes were so low, I was hoping she didn't fall asleep. I was trying my hardest not to make eye contact with anybody or burst out laughing. I could have smacked myself. What were we thinking? We should have just stopped at one.

I was fine with one. Now my mind was going back to one hour ago when I felt less high and wishing I could go back to then. I was so high right then; I had to snap out of it. Everything seemed to slow down; why was everybody talking so slow?

"G.B., G.B." (G.B. is what my coaches and teammates called me.) I snapped out of it to realize they were calling my name. I jumped up and put my hand in the middle. "Lady Tygers on 3: 1, 2, 3, Lady Tygers." We started walking up the stairs to line up. I stopped just before I hit the second to last step at the top. The cheerleaders and the JV team were standing on both sides of the stairs, forming a tunnel.

My team was starting to get amped up; some were bouncing up and down, the JV team started their clap. The announcer said,

"Get on your feet for your Lady Tygers." The beat dropped for 3:6 mafias "who run it;" the fog machine went off and no one could see us as yet. The energy around us was building up.

I dribbled the ball and I ran out, leading my team through the fog. As I emerged through the fog I turned left and I was coming around the corner when I realized damn it, I went the wrong way. *Ok, ok, you're fine; just go with it. Maybe nobody noticed.* I rounded the next corner and crossed back across the court which led us into our layup drill. I made the layup and ran to the back of the rebound line.

The cheerleaders were standing on the sideline and Bianca grabbed my arm and whispered in my ear, "Are you high?" I burst out laughing. I couldn't hold it in anymore and she pushed me and said, "You are. What the hell were you thinking?" I said I wasn't and ran off to rebound as she stood there and shook her head.

As I waited in the line to get the ball to do another layup, I watched as my PNC went up for a layup. She looked fine at first and then *whomp,* the ball went over the backboard. What the heck was she doing? She rarely ever missed a layup, let alone throw it over the backboard. Maybe people would think she was just playing around. And I looked at Bianca's face and I could tell she knew as she stood there, still shaking her head. I grabbed my PNC by the arm after my layup and said, "Man, you have to pull yourself together before we get caught."

She said "All right, all right" and we both burst out laughing and went back to finishing drills.

The game started and what happened next was nothing short of amazing. I was a darn good passer—that was my thing, to "assist"—but I was doing stuff I didn't even know I could do and almost every pass connected, every last one! My PNC was hitting threes from half court and we were running this team effortlessly and I was thinking that maybe we should play high more often.

The game ended and all I could do was sigh in relief. We survived and I came down from my high. Man, was I hungry! I went home, ate, showered and went to bed.

The next day, people were giving dap and high fives, saying that it was a good game. It was still funny that we played so well, considering we were high out of our minds. But please don't attempt to do what we did. Getting high is not cool. Later that day I was called to the gym, which was weird, because I was not even supposed to be in gym in that grading period.

I walked in and three of our coaching staff were sitting there. What the heck were they doing there? My head coach said, "I have to ask you something and don't lie to me." I assessed the situation and I could tell by the look on her face that I was in trouble. I saw a brown paper bag beside her and assumed it was probably a drug test, but how did she know? I couldn't think of a way out of this situation. She asked, "Were you high in the game last night?"

I exhaled and said, "Yes."

She was pissed! "G.B., why would you do something like that?"

I thought, *Why else? Because I like to get high, obviously.* But I didn't dare say that to her so I just shrugged and said, "I don't know."

"Who was with you? Who else got high with you?"

"Nobody," I replied, "I was by myself."

"We already know that you weren't alone."

"Yes, I was," I responded. She then proceeded to tell me that what happened next was out of her hands because someone already reported their suspicions to the principal. *Are you freaking kidding me! Who told the principal?* I was screaming in my mind. She went on to tell me how serious this was and that we had to go to the principal's office.

CHAPTER 12

Once we were inside the principal's office, he told me how serious this was and that as of right now I was suspended pending an expulsion hearing. And in that moment, I knew I was dead. My mom hadn't killed me thus far, even though she wanted to sometimes. But I knew this would push her over the edge. She was going to kill me! Once I heard expulsion I stopped listening because I began to plan my own funeral in my head.

I got home that afternoon and saw that the school had been trying to call my house. Delete, delete, delete. I plopped down on the couch in the living room and thought to myself, *Ok, I can breathe a little; my mom isn't home yet.* The phone rang and it was one of our male coaches. He asked to speak with my mom and I said, "No."

He said, "Jamihla, put one of your parents on the phone."

I said, "Nah" and hung up. I truly didn't have a care in the world right then, and not in a good way. Neither one of them were home then, but he didn't know that, plus he got on my nerves. He thought because he knew my stepdad, that meant something. Naw dude, that meant nothing to me! The phone rang again and I answered, "Hello" as if I didn't know it was him. He started talking really strong and fast. "Jamihla, they are going to find out one way or another." I chose 'another' and hung up. I was definitely dead now. Good thing I stopped caring about stuff years ago.

My mom finally made it home and asked why I was not at practice. I thought, *No sense in prolonging the inevitable.* So, I told her everything. When she found out about me not being eligible to play the previous year, she was mad. When I lied to her and stayed out partying all night, she was beyond mad. So, I was not sure what to call what she was displaying right now.

I had never seen her that mad and lately I was making a sport out of it. I thought her head was literally going to explode. Her face turned red and she was cussing me out, and I'm pretty sure she invented some new words that day. Now I'd become a master of not letting things get to me but she cussed me out so bad that I actually started to feel like a piece of crap and I didn't like it, I didn't like it at all. Granted, I did play in a basketball game high, I did get suspended, and I might be expelled soon. But in my mind, I was just a dumb kid who made a mistake; the school was overreacting. My mom was definitely over reacting and regardless of all the hell that I'd caused, I didn't have to take this. So that left only one thing for me to do. I would tell my grandma. Regardless of what I did, my grandma always had my back.

For some reason even though we were suspended our coach still made us travel with the team. We weren't allowed to dress and we had to sit behind the team, not with the team "Whatever." The next day we had a game out of town.

While we waited on the bus, I used this time to call my grandmother and told her everything. She explained to me why what I did was wrong but she thought my mom's reaction was even worse. My grandmother was livid. She told me she would pick me up from the school when we got back. That gave me a sense of relief because my mom was still fuming with me.

Side note: people, do not allow your children to manipulate their grandparents against you or anyone else for that matter. You are the parent and what you say goes.

Back to the story; on the bus ride to the game no one talked to us, I mean no one. The other girls on our team were pissed and trying to make it very clear that they were ignoring us. I could understand being mad but the way they were acting was ridiculous. They were acting like little kids, like we were invisible.

At first, I was annoyed but then it became comical. I already felt like it was me against the world and for all I cared, they didn't have to say another word to me. I didn't care about anything; maybe I was a bad seed. We got back to the school after watching them lose. And just like she said she would be, my grandmother was there waiting. I got into the car and she drove to my house. She went in and talked to my mom and told her that she thought it would be best if I came and stayed with her for a few days.

I went inside and packed some clothes, and my mom didn't say anything to me. She just stared at me like she didn't know where she went wrong as I shut the door behind me to go get back in the car with my grandma. I was 17 years old and three quarters of the way through my senior year of high school. As we drove away, I had no idea if I would even be allowed to finish high school. I had no idea what the future held for me but what I did know was that would be the last day I would live at home with my mom.

Staying at my grandma's house was nothing new to me because I spent many nights there before. My grandmother was raising three of my little cousins because one of my aunts passed away. Sharese and Baby T were only toddlers and Sharell was a baby when she passed. We all got along but they were spoiled and sometimes it showed. But regardless of how they were acting on any given day, I loved them like little sisters.

The one thing that was really hard for me was not having my baby brother there. I was used to seeing him every day and he still snuck in my room every night when my mom went to sleep. I think our parents gave up on trying to stop him. I used to wonder if he was scared or felt alone and I always hoped my other little brother was being nice to him, because they would fight sometimes. Every time my baby brother would see me, he would always ask, "Are you coming home today?" And every time I told him no I felt like my heart was breaking looking into his little sad eyes.

My expulsion hearing was coming up in a few days and I had no idea what all it entailed. I had never been in trouble like this before in school. It would suck to make it this far and not be able to graduate. I thought this was so stupid and they were taking this way too far. Kids were high in school all the time; they were acting like I was the first kid to play high in a game. Was I?

The day of judgment came and I didn't think I really had any expectations. It was almost like I did what I did, so it was what it was. My mother was there with me and she was no longer angry—disappointed maybe, but I didn't think she had the desire to kill me anymore.

We walked into the principal's office and he was in there with one of the vice principals and an attorney for the school. The vibes in the room were sketchy. I looked at them and I knew they had already made up their minds and had every intention of expelling me. The first thing the attorney for the school said was they needed to speak to me alone. Um, what law school did he go to? Because I was a minor and that definitely was not going to happen, 'dip weed'. My mom replied, "Absolutely not!" You could tell that they were super annoyed and couldn't wait to get rid of me.

They started with what codes of conduct I violated and what school rules I broke and I began to see quickly where this thing was headed. Did I believe I deserved to be punished? Yes, because I accepted the fact that I was wrong, but wasn't being suspended from school and the team enough? I had already been out five days; I was being ostracized by my so-called teammates. What else did you people want from me? A blood sacrifice? To expel me would just be overkill!

My thoughts were broken up by a knock on the door. The principal said, "Come in" and the secretary poked her head in and said that there was representation here for Ms. Young.

The attorney turned and said, "Representation?" as my favorite big cousin Sheryl and my Aunt Neil entered the room.

Sheryl walked in with a legal pad and said, "I'm here for Ms. Young on behalf of Joan Day (my grandmother)." Oh, did I forget to mention earlier that my grandmother was the Vice President of the school board of education? The atmosphere completely changed. They even sat up a little straighter. After talking amongst themselves for a few seconds they told me that I could resume regular classes on Monday, and I could go back and play on the team for tournaments after my five-game suspension was up. The looks on their faces were priceless.

Walking out of that office, I knew the only reason I wasn't expelled was because of my grandmother and her representative! I knew I probably had a target on my back now so I should try to steer clear of trouble.

For the first couple of days my PNC and I were back we couldn't go to our classes. It was really weird; we just roamed the halls, hung out in the gym, and sat in our coach's classroom. No one said anything to us and it still felt like we were suspended, even though we were allowed to come back to school. After a few days things kind of went back to normal; however, some of the chicks on the team were still giving us the silent treatment.

Upon returning we also found out who snitched on us; it was one of our own teammates! What kind of shady, two-faced mess is that? We didn't hurt anybody; it didn't affect how we played in a bad way. Why in the world would you ever feel the need to snitch on your teammate? That was when I realized it will be the person standing right next to you that will stab you in the back. We couldn't beat her up; even though she almost got us kicked out of school permanently, she was still our teammate. So, we just unloaded six dozen eggs on her car one night.

The last night of my five-game suspension fell on senior night but my coach spoke with the principal and got them to approve for me to come back early. I thought that was really cool of her. My mother and grandma walked me across the floor on senior night as I would be taking the court for the last time in Pete Henry gymnasium. A few months after, we had prom and then senior year came to an end.

Woo hoo! Thank you, Jesus! I made it out—barely, but I made it. I was finally free and I could leave this place and all the high school drama behind me. There was no better feeling than walking across that stage and having my grandmother hand me my diploma. That will be a day I will never forget. That also put "THE END" stamp on high school. And just like everybody who graduates, I took a deep breath and thought, *Ah, I'm grown now, no more rules, no more going to bed early. From now on everything is about what I want to do.* And that's exactly what I did: everything I wanted to do.

CHAPTER 13

When summer started most of my days were filled with getting high. My older cousin always had weed and any time I would go over to his house he would throw me an ounce just to keep his friends from trying to smoke with me. We were fresh out of high school so we were fresh meat for all the older dudes who were borderline predators. Aubrey was already messing with a dude a few years older than her who was also messing with one of my other friends, and there was always some drama but that's another story. Bianca couldn't have cared less about a dude; she was in a relationship and she was happy.

At this time, I decided I didn't really want to date anybody. I knew my cousin would kill any of his friends who tried to talk to me. And the dudes my age were still so obnoxious. I had lost all respect for men growing up, from seeing my mom and aunt being physically abused by men who supposedly loved them. I never understood it; I remember being a kid and thinking, *How can such strong women put up with this?*

I remember being a little girl and feeling helpless as I watched my mom run for her life, crying and screaming, trying to get away from my brother's dad. I remember wishing I could kill him. I wanted him dead but I just stood there and I don't remember crying but I do remember every bit of hate I felt for him.

I remember watching all the women in my family run the household while men did whatever they wanted. My stepdad never mistreated me but I never saw him hold down a steady job. He got mixed up in drugs and all he and my mother would do was argue. I remember thinking what was the point of marriage if the woman had to carry all the weight. I had friends whose parents were married but their dads were trying to get with girls my age.

I never once saw a man in his role as God intended, being the head of the household, being the protector and the provider. All the men I ever saw growing up were driven by lust, money, or drugs. And I knew I wasn't going to become one of the women who put up with it. It seemed like the men were living the good life while the women were burdened with all the responsibilities.

Everyone my age seemed to be obsessed with sex and I guess after all the stuff that happened when I was younger, I just wasn't that interested. My friend helped me get a little factory job and I worked from 6:00 AM to 2:00 PM. It was cool for the moment and the work was super easy. But every day I would look around and think, *I'm not ending up like these people.*

Don't get me wrong; people have to make a living and I have a lot of respect for people who can stand on a line and work day in and day out. But I thought there had to be more to life than that. Eventually I got bored with that and took a job where my grandmother worked. I was working with one of the youth programs with first and second graders. Kids that age are hilarious; you never know what they're going to say and they're so full of energy.

A lot of nights Aubrey and I would hang out and smoke. We would put a towel under the door to my room and crack the window and sit and smoke and people watch. One night, I don't know if it was because we were so high or just the ridiculousness of the situation that made us laugh to the point where I couldn't breathe.

We were staring out the window halfway through a blunt and it was like 2:00 AM. A yellow taxi pulled up and it was parked waiting for someone to come out, obviously. We saw my little cousin Baby T, my little brother, and one of my other little cousins get in the cab, and it took off. Their ages ranged from 13-14; Aubrey and I looked at each other and we hit the ground rolling. Where in the hell were they going, and in a cab, for that matter? Tears were rolling down our faces. They looked so suspicious, if I hadn't been so high, I would have probably gone and said something to my grandma. But I was too high and I couldn't stop laughing and to this day every time I think about it, I crack up and wonder where in the heck they went in that taxi in the middle of the night.

Aubrey and I always had moments like this where all we did was laugh. She and Bianca would be leaving soon for college and I would miss these days. August rolled around and Bianca and Aubrey were gone. I enrolled in OSU Mansfield and my first class didn't start for a few more weeks. I wasn't feeling going back to school at all. I had just gotten out of high school and now I was going right back into school—the thought of it made me sick to my stomach.

Just like every year, this was no different. At the end of the summer it was time for the annual Brooks & Holmes tournament. This was a big basketball tournament held every year in honor and remembrance of two local basketball players who were killed in a car accident on their way back to college. Teams from all over would come and compete. There would always be a DJ and food trucks. And the whole city would come out in support. Dudes would circle the park trying to show off their cars or their new sound systems. It was always live at Johns Park during tournament time.

This year would be special, though. It was the first time they would have all girl teams facing off. Most of the girls who would be playing were from the high school, former and current. I would be starting point guard on my team and we had some of the best players from the past couple years playing today. I still loved the game of basketball and it was still a place I found peace, so I was ready for it. We practiced a few times together and now it was time for the game.

There was a different type of excitement in the air and the park was packed with people. Waiting for the game to start, I walked around the park and talked to a few people here and there. As I walked, I noticed this dude staring at me, everywhere I went. I felt like he was watching me. I felt like I remembered him from somewhere but for the life of me, I couldn't figure out where. I passed him several times and each time he was just staring at me. I still couldn't remember where I knew him from.

Finally, it was about thirty minutes until we played and ten minutes before they started the clock to warm up. My cousin Jason came up to me and said, "Hey cuz, come with me. I want to introduce you to someone." Jason was my cousin on my dad's side; I met him when I was younger and he and his brothers had always checked in on me.

I walked with him to the other side of the park and we were heading straight toward the guy that kept staring at me. I was thinking maybe Jason told him something about me or he knew I was Jason's little cousin and that was why he had been staring. So, we walked over to him and the guy stretched his hand out to shake mine and said, "Hello Jamihla, nice to meet you." As he shook my hand he said, "I'm Michael; I'm your dad."

What did this nigga just say? He continued to ramble on about something and my mind couldn't even process what was happening? *What does he mean he's my dad? Who is this guy, and why is he here? Is this a joke? This has to be some sick joke. Who shows up thirteen years later talking about, "I'm your dad?" Dude, they said you left when I was four years old! Why are you here now? This has to be a joke. Where have you been?*

His voice broke through my thoughts and I heard him saying something about he heard how good I was at basketball and how proud of me he was and I zoned out again. I'd walked past this dude several times and he decided that right now was the time he needed to talk to me, before my game—what a selfish prick. I didn't know what this dude expected me to say.

I saw my team walking to the court. I told him that I had to go and as if this wasn't already awkward enough, before I turned to walk away, he looked me dead in the eyes and said, "You know I love you, right?" I turned and walked away in utter disbelief. "You know I love you, right?"

What type of crap is that to say to someone when you've been MIA for thirteen years?! No calls, no letters, not even a birthday card! "You know I love you, right?" How in the hell would I know he loved me? This dude had to be crazy. I made it inside the fences to the basketball court, and my mind was everywhere but on the game.

We warmed up for a while and it was time for tip-off. The jump ball was up and it was tipped in our favor. I caught the ball and I was dribbling down court. I saw one of my teammates cutting toward the basket. I quickly threw a no-look pass; she caught it and tossed it off the glass: two points. People were cheering. I looked over and saw this dude and he was cheering. I shook my head. "Get back on defense."

I backpedaled; the ball was on the other side of the court. One of the players on the other team pulled up; it bounced off the rim. We had the ball; I ran down the court. I went to the right corner outside the three-point line. The ball was passed to me; I pulled up—*swoosh*—bottom of the net. I looked over and the crowd was cheering and I saw this dude giving people high fives. "That's my daughter, that's my daughter!"

And it's hard to describe it but in that moment, it was like something literally broke in me. My body slowed down as I tried to get back on defense. She beat me and the other team scored. I was dribbling down court telling myself, "Focus, focus." I swung the ball to the left. My teammate caught it; she took a shot; she scored.

Next time down I lost my dribble and turned the ball over. Dang it! The time after that my teammate was open; I passed the ball and it was picked off (turnover). I was beat getting back on defense; other team scored. *Ugh, what is happening?* I'm screaming to myself. I looked over and I saw this dude and heard him yelling, "It's all right, you'll get it back. Let's go; you got this." *What is he doing? He doesn't even know me; who does he think he is cheering for? Me?*

I needed to sit down. I put my hand up to come out. I went back in the second half and my head was still not in the game. This was the worst game I had ever played and still I could hear him cheering. The game finally ended and I felt so defeated.

After the game there was more of him acting like he was my dad. He told me that he wanted to keep in touch but we didn't even exchange numbers. And on that day, I walked away from that park with an open wound that I didn't even know I had all these years, and I never picked up a basketball again.

CHAPTER 14

Growing up I always wanted locs (dreadlocks) but my mom would never let me do it to my hair; she always told me I had to wait until I was older. Now I made my own decisions and I decided I was locking my hair. It took hours to get my hair sectioned off and twisted, but the hairdresser finally finished and it was time to see my new look. I looked in the mirror and was like *What did I just do to myself?* She explained to me that everybody has to go through the busted phase and as I looked in the mirror, 'busted' was my thought exactly.

On the weekends, nine times out of ten you could catch us at Alexis' house, and we always had fun. There was a core group of us but there were always different people that would stop through to 'kick' it with us. There would always be a couple of bottles of liquor and beer, the smell of weed would be in the air, and a black-and-mild or two would always be passed around. And you most certainly could always catch a game of spades going on. We would always start at Alexis' house and then end up at one of the local bars around 12:30-1:00 AM. Then we would be back to do it all over again the next weekend.

Around this time my grandma had moved us from the north end to the suburbs right next to an elementary school. It was cool but it was different than what we were used too. My little cousins really had a hard time adjusting because all their friends lived in the same neighborhood we moved from. They hated being so far away from everything. I didn't mind it; I had my own space upstairs and I was grown now.

I had graduated and my grandmother allowed me to come and go as I pleased. She even gave me my own key to her SUV to use whenever I wanted to and to help run my little cousins around. And trust me, they always wanted to go somewhere. My cousin Montay was now living in the house that we moved out of and if I wasn't at Alexis' or work, I was over there at his house. I loved and looked up to Montay. People feared and respected him but he was one of the nicest people you could ever meet. Because of who he was, he always had a target on his back by the police. The police constantly harassed him. Don't get me wrong; they constantly harassed everybody but they had a special hatred for him. They acted like he was Scarface or somebody; it was crazy.

School started and I went to classes for a few weeks but soon realized my heart just wasn't in it. So a short time afterward, I stopped going altogether. Nobody ever even asked me why I stopped going, which I thought was kind of weird; maybe they just thought I was old enough to make my own decisions too. Once I decided I was done with school that left more time for me to do me, and do me I did.

My only interest right now was making money and kicking it. I was still getting high whenever I wasn't at work but it wasn't the same as before. Instead of always finding everything funny I started to find myself deep in thought. My cousin Montay was now on the run because of a bunch of stuff that went down at his house, and he was the one taking the fall for it. He had always been in and out of jail from as far back as I could remember, and I always missed him when he was gone. It was even worse this time because we had grown so close; he was like a big brother and I was just hoping he was ok.

One morning I was walking back to my room after getting out of the shower, and I heard Montay's voice coming through a speaker. I thought, *Who's in my room?* I got to the top of the stairs and saw that two of my cousins had found their way into my room and were counting money. My room was kind of big because it had two sections; one part was like a small living room and the other part was a bedroom. The entire floor of the living room area was covered with stacks of money. I had never seen that much money in my life!

Looking back, I should have told them to get out of my room and take it somewhere else. But I didn't; instead, I got dressed spoke with Montay for a little and I was out the door. Alexis had made a new friend a little while back named Kelsey; she was the sister of one of her cousin's girlfriends. She had been trying to get me to kick it with them for a while and I had been busy lately so I never made it. But I promised I would link up with them tonight.

When I met Kelsey, I observed that she was really cool. I found out she was ten years older than me, moved here from Miami, and was a stripper. Leaving nice weather for Ohio didn't make sense to me but to each his own. Her career path, even though undesirable, seemed to be working out well for her. The night went on and there were a lot of laughs, a lot of drinks, and as Kelsey and I talked we learned a lot about each other.

Alexis said she was going to run and get some more weed, and everybody else said they wanted to ride with her. There wouldn't have been enough room for me, and I drove anyway. Alexis asked if I would be cool to stay and wait for them to get back. I looked at Kelsey and she said, "Yeah, the night's young." I told Alexis it was cool, I would chill for a minute, and they all got in the car and left.

Kelsey and I talked some more and had a few more drinks. She started asking me about my hair and then asked if she could touch it. I said, "Sure." She rolled the ends of my hair between her fingers and after a short while she started to run her fingers through it, starting at my scalp. We were already in her bedroom chilling because she was showing us something earlier. We were sitting on this huge white plush comforter and she just kept rubbing my hair. It started to make me sleepy on top of all the alcohol I had consumed. The way I was sitting on the bed my feet were dangling off so I just laid back to shut my eyes for a minute. Then out of nowhere she kissed me, and it wasn't like when Dominique did it. I was shocked but I was no longer trying to rationalize it in my head and I just went with it. She didn't stop and I can't say that I wanted her to.

This night was the first time I had sex with another woman and I imagined the experience was similar to when an addict had their first hit of a really powerful drug like crack or heroin or meth—you pick the poison you want to compare it to. Either way I was hooked, not on her but on that feeling I got. It was almost like a new sense of power, if that makes any sense. And this would be the start of a new chapter in my life. I didn't care anymore about what people thought; they had been calling me gay my whole life. And now I finally believed them and there was no turning back.

CHAPTER 15

Over the next couple of months Kelsey and I became really close friends. She would have me come sit at the strip club while she worked at night, and we would chill most of the day if I wasn't at work. Around this time, I also started talking to Anna, one of the seniors at the high school. I knew her from back in the day. We ran into each other one night and exchanged numbers; it seemed like we would talk for hours some days. I didn't know yet how Anna would fit into my life but I was sure time would tell.

It had been a few months since all my friends had left for college. One of my best friends was home and Kelsey was having a party at her house that night. I thought it would be a good time for her and Kelsey to meet. I went and picked my friend up around 8:00 PM. As we drove to the party, she was telling me all about school and I was telling her about Kelsey.

We got to the house and you could hear the music from the street. When we walked in, the party was in full swing already. Kelsey ran over, jumped on me and kissed me. I introduced the two of them. Kelsey was being her happy, bubbly self and my friend smiled and said, "Nice to meet you." Kelsey ran off to go talk to other people and I got my friend and me a drink. People were asking her how school was going and stuff like that, and she seemed to be enjoying herself.

After a few hours, the party was still going on like it was never going to end and everybody seemed to be having a great time except my friend. I noticed that she was sitting off in the corner to herself. I asked her what was wrong and she replied, "Nothing." I knew she was lying though, because it was written all over her face. I asked her if she was ready to go and she said, "Yes." I told Kelsey I would be back and I left to take my friend home.

When we walked outside it was raining so we ran to the car. The mood in the car was so much different than when I picked her up earlier that night. She was staring out the window, not even looking at me. I tried to replay the night in my head and thought over what could have happened. Did I do something to make her mad? I thought back to all the people I saw talking to her and came up with nothing. I called her name and she didn't respond, as if she was deep in thought. I said her name again and she responded, "What?"

I asked, "What is wrong with you? What happened?"

She looked at me and started crying. *What the hell is happening right now?* was all I could think. And now her face was in her hands and she was crying harder. I didn't know what to do and it was actually scaring me. I didn't think I'd ever seen her like this before. I pulled over and parked on the side of the road and grabbed her arm, pulling her hand away from her face. "What is wrong with you? Why are you crying? Did someone do something to you?"

"No," she said through tears.

I asked, "What is wrong with you then?"

She said, "I can't—I'm really confused now."

"You can't what?" I asked.

"I can't do this" she said.

"Do what?" What in the hell was she talking about?

She looked at me, eyes full of tears, and yelled, "I'm in love with you!"

I looked her dead in her eyes and said, "No you're not" and she said, "Yes I am, I'm in love with you," while she continued to cry. "I'm in love with you and I hated seeing you with her."

Why me? Why now? We had been friends all these years and not once had she ever acted like she liked me in that way! She was just confused; she had to be drunk right now. I didn't know what to do with this. I loved her but she was my best friend and she was crying and telling me she was in love with me. She wouldn't stop crying and I didn't know what else to do so I kissed her, and she kissed me back, and I didn't stop until she stopped crying. We got to her house and we sat and talked in the car for what seemed like forever. When she finally went into the house, I sat in the car and thought, *What in the hell am I going to do now?* I loved hanging out with Kelsey but this was my best friend, you know.

I headed back to Kelsey's feeling torn and having no idea what I was going to do next. What I did know was that my friend would be going back to school soon so I made up my mind that I would talk to her tomorrow about what happened tonight. Why couldn't anything in my life ever be simple?

Morning rolled around and I went over my friend's house so we could talk about the night before. She said that she remembered everything and that she wasn't drunk. I asked her if she was sure that was how she really felt about me and she said, "Yes."

I told her, "Why don't you see how you feel when you get back to school and we'll go from there." I really wanted her to process what she was saying and how she was feeling and make sure it wasn't just some jealousy type thing. She left for school a couple of days later and I was supposed to drive down and get her in a couple of weeks.

Meanwhile Kelsey and I were still spending almost every day together. She gave me a key to her house so I could come and go as I pleased, and everything was going great until one night I told her I couldn't stay out all night. I had to help my grandmother put up signs for one of the judges running for reelection. I told her that I would be by after I was done with that. She was upset and didn't understand why I couldn't just get up in the morning and go, and I explained to her if I stayed there would be no getting up and going in the morning. I left her angry but what could I do?

I helped my grandmother put up the signs the next morning like she asked me to and afterward I dropped her off and went to Kelsey's. It was about 10:30 in the morning when I arrived at Kelsey's. I walked in and saw people passed out on the couch from the night before. They must have kicked it hard.

I walked up the stairs and opened the door to the room and one of the dudes that usually kicked it with us popped out of the bed with a look of panic in his eyes. He was staring at me and I saw she was still sleeping next to him. I slid her key off my key ring and tossed it on the bed.

She woke up and was looking at him like *what happened* and she turned and looked at me as I turned to walk away. She screamed, "Jamihla, wait, let me explain!" But my mind was made up. I was done. I kept walking and she chased me down the stairs, "Please, please wait." I hit the door before she made it to the bottom of the stairs. As I shut the door to the car, I knew that was the last time I would see Kelsey.

She called me over and over again for the next couple weeks but I ignored her every time. I didn't know what she actually thought she would be able to say to change things. Either way, I wasn't trying to hear it and eventually the calls stopped.

CHAPTER 16

When my friend came back from school she asked about Kelsey and I told her whatever we had was over. She told me she was sure who she wanted and it was me. I was still skeptical about it but oh well, why not?

Over the next couple of months, I would take trips to pick her up and drop her off at school. We would chill on the weekends and always have fun; I mean, it was easy because we were already friends in the first place.

One weekend I went to pick her up and things were just off. My drive took longer than usual and when I got there something just didn't feel right. She buzzed me into her dorm and I walked up the stairs to the hallway that led to her room. She would talk about her roommate from time to time but I had never met her. Today she was there and my friend introduced us and instantly in my gut I knew this girl had a crush on her.

Nothing was said; I couldn't even say she looked at her a certain way. I just knew. Deep down inside, I knew. I started wondering if she knew this girl liked her too. How could she not? I wasn't even there five minutes and I could tell. This whole encounter just seemed weird. My friend was not quite ready to go; she was still putting stuff in her bag so I ran to get my drink out of the car because she could take a while.

I ran into a couple of dudes I went to high school with outside and we talked for a minute and then I continued to my car to grab my drink. I went back and somebody was coming out so I didn't have to be buzzed in.

I went back up the stairs to her room and the door was locked. "What the hell! She knew I was coming right back." I knocked on the door—nothing. I knocked again and I heard, "Here I come." *Man, what in the hell is going on? The room is the size of a sardine can; what does she mean here she comes? If you stand up, you're literally at the door.* I started getting hot, which I noticed happened a lot when I got mad. First my hands got really hot, then my face, then my ears. Time was ticking by. What the hell was she doing that was taking so long? Man, something wasn't right. My ears were burning now.

"Forget this." I went down the stairs and as I hit the bottom step, I heard the door at the top open, and it was her. She had the nerve to ask, "Where are you going?"

"What in the hell do you mean where am I going? What were you doing that took you so long to open the door?"

She didn't answer my question but asked, "Why are you so mad?"

"What do you mean why am I so mad? You left me in the hall knocking forever." She told me that I was tripping, and for some reason that pissed me off even more and I saw red. I took off up the stairs and she took off running down the hall toward her room. She made it to her room before I got to her. I don't even know what I would have done if I had caught her.

I went outside to cool off and I thought to myself, *What is happening to you? This is not you!* Even if something was going on between them, in the past, I would be upset but I also would just easily walk away from people. This was something different though, and I didn't like it. After I cooled off, I went and sat in my car. I called her and she ended up coming downstairs with her stuff.

On the way home we talked and she assured me nothing was going on. I don't even think I cared at that point. I didn't like who I was becoming; there were too many feelings involved here. We dated for a few more weeks and then realized our friendship was more important.

Anna and I were still talking on the phone a lot and when she wasn't at school or work, she would hang out with me. We were growing closer and granted, she was 18 but she was still in high school so things had their limitations. She couldn't hang out everywhere I was or stay out as late as me. She had to be off the phone by 9:00 PM on school nights. Her stepdad was a complete psycho; he would come in her room at night when we were on the phone and she would quickly put her phone under her pillow. You would hear muffled talking and sometimes the call would end.

That crap was weird as hell and she always seemed so scared of him. I would always ask her why she wouldn't say something to her mom, and she would always act as if it didn't matter. I hated the dude and I knew he had a sick infatuation with his stepdaughter, but she would never say much about what was going on. We would spend time watching movies, going to games, and smoking.

I was already selling weed around this time, and the guy I was getting it from had already given me my first gun. It was a small .25 Beretta that I could easily conceal when I was out and when I was home, I kept it tucked away in a little hidden compartment in the wall in my room. Anna would ask a lot of questions about how I got into selling weed and my experiences with other chicks. She would also ask me about different rumors she heard, and I would tell her what was the truth and what were lies. I could tell the more we talked the more curious she was becoming.

CHAPTER 17

One day we were chilling and she started asking random questions again, but this time she asked how I felt about her. This wasn't the first time she asked me something like this and I told her before that I found her attractive. But there was something different about how she asked this time. It was more like she wanted me to want her, and at this point, after all the conversations and chilling together, I did. She continued to talk and I leaned over and kissed her. I thought she would be shocked and I was waiting for her to pull back but she didn't; she kissed me back and within a couple of minutes, things escalated to the next level between Anna and me.

Things between us continued for a few months My friends knew what was up because she was always around or we would be on the phone when I was around them. Her friends suspected stuff but I don't think they ever really knew. And I didn't mind; that was something hard to admit, especially in high school. Hell, I struggled with people calling me that in high school when I wasn't even messing with women.

I hadn't even told my mom anything about my life yet but I'm sure she had her suspicions. What I did have a problem with though, was when we decided to become exclusive. There were things she didn't want me to do and for the most part I respected her wishes. She couldn't be out with me all the time because she was still in school and I kicked it a lot so I tried to respect some of her wishes. But I started hearing rumors about her hanging out with this dude Ryan. She denied it until she was blue in the face but one thing, I've always been good at is knowing when someone is telling a lie. And she was telling me a bald-faced lie. Once you lie to me there's really no coming back from that. I hadn't caught her yet so I just played along for the time being.

People would call or text me anytime they saw them as much as talking to each other. It was kind of comical; her friends would tell my friends stuff because they said they were tired of her lies. There was a rule I set for myself after I started messing with Kelsey. The first time any chick I was sleeping with was found to be messing with somebody else, it was a wrap.

These dudes around here were hoes and messed with everybody and besides, I had male friends and you wouldn't believe some of the stuff they were doing. For example, giving a chick a STD so she would have to go to the doctor and get the medicine so he could split it with her. Like what in the world kind of sick crap is that? Yeah, if I found out you were messing with someone else, it was a wrap. I'm not catching nothing for nobody. I don't care how good you look.

I let her think everything was good between us because I knew I would catch her soon enough. Like I was telling you earlier, every time someone who knew me would see them as much as talking, I would get a text or a call. This summer was no different than any other summer. If it was nice out people would be at Johns Park hooping or watching pickup games.

I had just gotten dressed and was headed to link up with my friend Shawna when I got a call on my cell phone. It was one of my homies telling me they were at the park and they just saw Anna with Ryan. Like I said, I already knew what the deal was but I like catching people red-handed. I was meeting Shawna at her cousin's house who lived around the corner from the park so I decided to ride by.

I had spoken with Anna on the phone and she knew I was

going to hang with Shawna so I knew she wouldn't anticipate me riding past the park. I hit the corner and rode down the street where all the cars were parked at the park. I saw Ryan's car parked up the street. I scanned the park for Anna and I didn't see her, but I knew she was there. I saw the homie that called me and he nodded in the direction of Ryan's car. I gave a nod back to say 'good looking out' and rolled down the street toward the car. I pull up right next to his car, and lo and behold who is sitting in the passenger seat—Anna. He saw me before she did and I saw his mouth move and she turned around. I gave her a head nod like 'what's up' and the look on her face was priceless! You would have thought she saw a ghost. She started to get out of the car and I just shook my head and laughed and pulled off. She knew she was caught; she told me she didn't even talk to this dude.

My phone started ringing. It was Anna. I ignored it. I was at the stop sign getting ready to turn toward Shawna's cousins house when I looked in the rear view and saw this broad flying up behind me. "How did she get to her car that fast?" I took off and she started blowing my phone up. I didn't answer. I don't know what she thought was going to happen. I went the opposite way now because I didn't want her to know where I was going.

She knew I was going to hang with Shawna but she didn't know where. *She'll turn off soon enough*, I thought to myself and started heading toward the other side of town. My phone kept ringing. *Ugh, stop calling me.* I started to go faster but she kept up. *This darn broad, man!* I started hitting alleys and side streets. My phone kept ringing. I finally answered. "Man, stop calling me."

Did I forget to mention she had a slight anger problem? She yelled into the phone, "Then pull the f**** over!" I hung up and kept driving. I think I lost her between Bowman and 6th street so I headed back to meet up with Shawna.

I finally got to my destination and Shawna and her people

were standing outside. I stepped out of the car and Anna came down the street doing like 50 mph in a 25-mph zone and almost ran me over. "What the hell!"

She parked and got out of the car as I was walking up the grass to go into the house. She yelled, "Jamihla, stop being stupid and let me talk to you."

Shawna and her people were dying laughing. I told her, "Go on, man; ain't nothing for us to talk about" and I walked into the house.

When Shawna and her cousin came in the house they were still laughing and were like, "Man, what did you do to that girl?"

I replied, "Nothing, she did it to herself."

A few days later I ended up letting her say her piece even though I knew that I was done. She swore up and down it wasn't what I thought, which was irrelevant to me at this point. She asked me to take her back by the park to give Ryan his necklace. But wait a minute. Why did she have his necklace if it wasn't like that? You tell me. Regardless, out of the kindness of my heart I took her up by the park.

He was standing outside his car as we pulled up and I got out. I leaned up against my car and he looked at me and said, "Hey Jamihla, I didn't know. Are we good? You can have her."

I laughed. "Naw, I'm good. I don't want her; that's all you, G." We went back and forth like this for about 30 seconds. Anna looked crushed and in this moment I did not care. After dealing with all of Anna's lies and bull crap—let me correct that; it was a combination of things but Anna was the straw that broke the camel's back. And I decided from that point on, a decade before it became a hit song, "These hoes ain't loyal and from now on I'm going to treat them as such."

CHAPTER 18

Whenever we needed a break from the field my cousin Shon and I would drive down to the Cap (Columbus, Ohio) to her sister's house for some much-needed rest and relaxation. We would just chill and get high all day, without a care in the world. I always felt refreshed when we came back from those trips.

I was still talking to Anna but it was purely recreational. My mind was on a whole different level, regardless of how she felt. We came back from one of our trips to the Cap after being gone for about two weeks. So I decided to drop in and see what Alexis and others were up to.

When I got there everybody was already kicking it. I asked what was up for the night and they said they were waiting on some pills. I knew they had been popping "x" lately but I never did it, and I can't recall being around when they actually did it either. There was this new chick they started hanging with, named Angela, and she was the one who was bringing the pills. I had heard a lot about her but had never met her. She finally arrived and she was fine. She was a little shorter than me, with long black hair, dressed like she just stepped out of a magazine. Alexis introduced us and we started talking and my phone started ringing. It was freaking Anna. I told Angela to excuse me, I was going to step outside and take this call really quick but I would be right back.

I stepped outside. "What's up?" *Man, ain't she supposed to be in bed?*

She heard the music and laughter coming from inside the house. She asked, "Where you at?" I told her Alexis's. She said,

"You better not get wasted tonight or I'm gone mess you up!"

"Um yeah, ok," I laughed.

"Jamihla, I'm not playing and you better not have no broads in your face!"

I laughed again as I was looking through the window at Angela. Anna started going off about something, maybe my lack of attention, maybe the fact that I kept laughing at everything she was saying. I don't know; either way, I was ready to go back inside and grab a drink.

Angela was motioning me through the window to come back. I got off the phone with Anna but not before she reiterated how I better not do this and I better not do that, and what she would do to me if I did. I was just replying, "Uh huh, uh huh," while I was thinking, *I'm definitely going to do that, that too and maybe that twice.* "All right, goodnight."

I went back into the house and over to Angela. She took out a little white pill with a Superman symbol on it and asked, "You want half?" I told her I'd never done that before and she proceeded to tell me everything that I would feel if I took it.

I told her, "I don't know, man; I hear people be tripping sometimes when they take those."

She said, "I swear I'll be with you the whole night; I won't let anything happen to you. It's just a half."

I'm not one to cave to peer pressure, never have been, but I was intrigued by this little white pill. So I said, "Give it to me" and she bit it in half super seductively.

I should have run then but I didn't, and she gave me the other half. They all told me not to leave because some people freak out when their high kicks in. I was like, "All right," and I popped it into my mouth. How bad could it be? Besides, I only took a half.

After finishing my beer, I went to pee and I still didn't feel anything. I was finishing up in the bathroom and I went to stand up and I fell back into the bathtub. What the hell? The whole world felt different! *What the hell! Wait! Get control of yourself; you are fine. I'm breathing.* Breathing felt so good. I was trying to suck in extra air; I loved the air! *Ok, ok, calm down. You are rolling. They told you about this; pull yourself together.* I fixed my clothes, adjusted my fitted hat, and walked out of the bathroom. Oh my God, dude! I felt so good.

I walked out and everybody else looked fine. I put my hands up on the entryway door panel between the living room and dining room. Alexis looked over at me and said, "You're rolling, aren't you?" I burst out laughing; I had never felt this good in my entire life. My friends said, "Let's go to this little block party"

I threw my keys to my PNC and said, "I'll walk," because the air felt so good.

They all started laughing and said, "You can't walk."

Angela said, "You are riding with me."

Man, she is so fine, I thought to myself as I said, "Yeah, I'm riding with you."

We went to the party and it was really just a bunch of people kicking it in the street, not necessarily a block party. Regardless, we still had a blast and we weren't even there that long. We left there and planned to meet up at the bar. Angela told them we would catch up in a minute. When we got in her car she said, "I want to show you something." I was down for anything she wanted that night.

We rode to the south end of town and I had no idea where we were going and I couldn't say that I really cared. She hit state route thirteen and took the 71S on ramp toward Columbus. She looked over and said, "Watch this." She opened the sunroof and hit about 80mph on the highway and kept climbing. The way the lights flashed and the way the air was hitting me was like nothing I've ever felt before in my life. It felt like my lungs were being massaged by silk. The way the lights ran together looked like some kind of crazy neon rainbow. She was smiling because I was sure she knew what I was feeling. We went up a few exits and then she turned around and headed back toward Mansfield.

There was one thing they left out when they were telling me about these pills. They left out the part about the tendency to say whatever you were thinking, which was something I already had a problem doing. I was already a cocky little something at this point, so there was no telling what was going to happen next. And one thing I did know about myself at this point was all I needed was a conversation. One conversation and I could get most women to do anything I wanted.

We got back to Mansfield and Angela said she had to stop and get something from her house. We pulled in the driveway and she looked over, smiling, and said, "Are you ok?"

I said, "Yeah, you know I'm going to screw you, right?" *Wait, what in the hell did I just say?* Yep, I said it! I just told this chick I was going to screw her. Whelp, can't take it back now that it's out. She giggled and stroked my face like I was a little kid or something. And as if I hadn't already said enough, I looked back at her and said "I'm serious, watch me."

She laughed and said, "Come on," and we went in her house.

She took me down some stairs into her basement. She had a nice little setup down there: a big screen TV and a huge sectional. We walked into this office she had down there and she told me to sit down. She picked up a video camera that was sitting on the desk and she scrolled for a minute and pressed play. She handed it to me and said, "Watch this." It was a video of her, let's just say, entertaining herself. My mouth dropped open. Was she really showing me this? So many red flags should have gone off but I was young, dumb and full of—you know the saying. As the video finished playing, I knew now more than ever that the statement I made in the car was true.

I met back up with my friends the next day and they asked what happened. I told them I was too high and had to lie down. They all started laughing like, yeah right! We chopped it up for a while about the night's events and then my PNC and I went to get some shells and food. (for those of you who don't know what shells are, they are cigars that people take and dig out the insides and replace with something else, typically weed.)

We lived off McDonalds's at this time, and we always got the same thing: a double cheeseburger and fries, and my PNC always had to get Big Mac sauce on hers. We got back to Alexis' house, fired up a blunt and by nightfall we were ready to party all over again.

CHAPTER 19

It had been a year since I graduated high school and I didn't really talk to my mom that much these days. I don't know if it was because I thought she would be mortified at what I had become, or if I was so caught up in doing me and self-gratification that I really didn't have time for anyone else. I felt like I lived life so long trying to please everyone else that my only focus in life right now was pleasing myself, and please myself I did.

Over the next several weeks Angela was around a lot more. We exchanged numbers the first night I met her and we had been talking ever since. She told me she had a boyfriend but she spent so much time chilling with us I wondered when she ever had time for this dude. Either way, I didn't care; I knew eventually I would have her. She would always joke that I was just a baby and too young for her. She was twenty-five and I was eighteen. I used to laugh and say, "Age ain't nothing but a number." Unless it's a minor, then you're just a sicko.

As time went on, Angela kind of became a part of the crew and was with us almost every day. We found ourselves going off more and more to talk. I still talked to Anna but like I said, the situation we had was dead; I couldn't trust that broad as far as I could throw her. I was starting to see a trend with women though; it was amazing how interested and in love they became when you were no longer an option. The week came and went and we decided to have a sleepover that weekend. Usually it was a mixed group of females and males when we kicked it but tonight it was only going to be the girls.

We were at my house. My grandma was out of town until Sunday and my little cousins were staying with their friends. We were actually supposed go back to Alexis' house but after a few drinks my friends started talking about when we used to hoop and one of them mentioned all the trophies in my room. Angela was like, "I want to see them; can I see them?"

I said, "Yeah, come on," and we walked up the stairs to my room. My room was all the way in the attic; it was like a loft. The awards were on the wall as you walked up the stairs. As you got to the top of the stairs there was a big table on the right that all my trophies sat on. Angela was looking at all my trophies and was like, "Dang, you must have really been good. Why didn't you go to school and play ball?"

I told her about all the stuff that happened in high school and how I fell out of love with the game. She was walking around the room as we were talking and we ended up in the bedroom part of it. I was standing in front of one of my dressers and she asked me what made me want to loc my hair. I told her how I had a mentor when I was young and I loved her hair and it made me want to loc mine. My mom would never let me do it so once I got old enough it was one of the first things I did, along with getting a couple tattoos.

She started running her fingers through my hair, and she was so close that I could smell her perfume. Man, she smelled like candy. Every inch of my body was tingling and we didn't even pop a pill tonight. She looked me in my eyes, and I said, "I thought I was too young for you."

She said, "Age ain't nothing but a number, remember" and we kissed. And it was as if everything around us disappeared. My friend's downstairs were forgotten for the moment.

The next hour was like something I had never experienced before and if my first time with Kelsey was like the first hit of crack for an addict, well, I'd just graduated to grade A 100% pure black tar heroin! When we finally went back downstairs everybody was already asleep so I didn't bother them. We just went back upstairs to my room and slept.

The next morning Alexis looked at me laughed, and started shaking her head. I looked at her and smiled and shrugged my shoulders. We got up and made breakfast: pancakes, eggs, sausage—you name it. Just as we were cleaning up, my grandmother walked in. She said good morning to everybody, and she already knew everyone except Angela, who didn't waste any time walking up to her and introducing herself. My grandmother said, "Nice to meet you" and asked if she could speak with me in the other room.

We went into the front room and sat on the couch and she said, "I'm not telling you what to do, but you need to be careful with that one."

I said, "What?"

She said, "That one, you need to be careful with." I said ok and started laughing and she looked at me and said, "Jamihla, I'm serious; you better hear me. You need to be careful with her."

I said, "Ok granny" and walked back into the other room. Listen, if a grandmother ever sits you down and tells you this about someone, if you don't listen to anything else I say, YOU NEED TO LISTEN TO THEM. This should have been a second red flag but again, I was young and dumb and full of—yeah, you remember.

Kicking it became a daily routine; if I was not at work, I was at Angela's house almost every night, and my little cousin Baby T and her best friend Nina were always over there with me. I must admit I was not the greatest role model then. One day I hope Baby T will forgive me for that, because I could see her becoming more and more like me. But again, I was so focused on myself that I was not thinking about leading her down the wrong path.

That's one thing I've learned over the years. There is always someone watching you, whether you are aware of it or not. Whether you want to be a role model or not, you have younger people paying attention to everything you're doing, so be careful what example you set.

Angela and I were always going out on the weekend and I could get into almost everywhere even though I was underage. Our favorite spot then was the VIP lounge. One night while we were there this dude Rel walked up to me. I knew him because I had smoked weed with him and some friends a couple of times about a year or two ago. He was like, "What's up Jamihla?"

I gave him a head nod and said, "What's up?"

He was like, "Hey, I know you're sleeping with my girl."

I'm like, "What!"

He said, "Yeah, I got cameras in the crib, but don't worry. I don't care or nothing; I was just telling you."

I felt sick to my stomach, not because he claimed it was his chick, but because he said he had cameras up in the house. I was like, *This dude has to be lying.*

He said, "I ain't mad; I'll be by there tomorrow to get what I have left over there."

I just played it off and said, "All right." *So this is the freaking boyfriend that's never anywhere to be found! Please God, don't let this dude be serious about having us on camera.*

I talked to Angela about it and she was all calm about it, like, "Yeah, he might; I never checked for them or anything, but that sounds like something he might do. Don't worry about it though. He's cool." Was this broad smoking rocks? "He's cool!" We're talking about freaking sex tapes! I was panicking inside. When we got back to her place, I looked over every inch of her house and found nothing. I was still sick to my stomach at the thought of it though. I stayed away from her house for a few days and she kept calling, insisting I was tripping. After a while nothing came of it, so I finally went back over there, despite the fact that this should have been red flag number three.

CHAPTER 20

We were kicking it so much at one point that sometimes I didn't even know what day it was. This little chick Tonya started hanging out with Baby T and Nina and started coming over when we were kicking it. She graduated a year after me and she seemed cool; I never had a problem with her. This dude Darnell was throwing a "Playas ball" and everybody knew him, so there was bound to be a bunch of people there.

The day of the party I and some of my friends went to the mall to do some last-minute shopping. I was just looking for accessories; I already had my outfit. I was wearing a brown fitted pantsuit with turquoise pin stripes, with a turquoise cami and some bad turquoise heels. I could switch it up when I wanted to. When I left the mall, I was going to go by and check on Angela since she hadn't answered her phone all morning. She had a dress to match my outfit but I wasn't sure if she needed anything else.

We left the mall and agreed to meet at Alexis' house later. I drove to Angela's and knocked on the door. It was locked, so after a few minutes I used my key. I figured she was probably passed out in the basement. The house was quiet. "Hey Angela, where are you?" No answer. I walked to the basement and started walking down the stairs "Ang..." and I saw the bed on the sofa couch pulled out and I saw Tonya sleeping. She was in lingerie and I saw Angela next to her. Angela jumped out of the bed and I saw she was in lingerie too. I said, "Oh my bad, I didn't mean to interrupt" and walked back up the stairs.

Angela was yelling, "Baby, wait; it's not what you think." Tonya woke up. I could hear Angela running up the stairs as I made it to the front door. But her chances of catching me were as likely as me catching feelings, and that wasn't happening. I saw her at the door as I was pulling out of the driveway and I threw up the deuce sign. I was laughing to myself as I was driving down the street calling Alexis to tell her what just happened. *These hoes wild, man,* I thought to myself. Alexis was like, "This has to be a lie—are you kidding me?"

"Nope, just left; crazy, ain't it?" We cracked up.

Angela was blowing my phone up but I was not even entertaining that. I needed to start getting ready for the party. I put my phone in the cup holder and I saw she left a voicemail. I would listen to it later. But right now, I had to go get fly, and I turned up T.I.'s "Let's get away." I went home and after a while I got dressed and went over Alexis' house and we all decided to go over Tay's before we headed out to the party. We took a couple of pictures and then we were off.

We got there and everybody was there and the party was, as kids would say today, "lit." And man! We kicked it hard; we danced so much that by the end of the night my feet were killing me. I didn't drink much because we were out on Park Avenue and the police were thick out there at night. When I left the party, I went home and changed into some basketball shorts and a t-shirt and got ready to lie down. I realized I had missed about thirty calls from Angela. Ok, so do you guys remember when I said if your grandmother ever tries to impart wisdom and says, "Be careful with this one" that you probably should listen? Well, right here was when I started to realize I should have listened to my grandmother.

I started listening to my messages and at first they were your typical messages when you catch somebody in the bed with someone else: "Please call me back; let me explain. Why aren't you answering? It's not what you think. Jamihla call me back. Maybe we should skip the party and just spend time talking tonight. Baby, please, I'm begging you, call me back. Why aren't you answering the f***ing phone? Ok, you win; I'm sorry. Call me back. So, I was thinking, maybe we could watch a movie and I would cook whatever you want. Let me know. Bye. I can't believe you went to the f***ing party. You know what, f**** it. I'm not calling again." She was literally calling while I was listening to these messages. I skipped through and went to the last message that she just left. Let me give you some context for what was about to happen.

Angela had a fascination with samurai swords and knives. They were everywhere in her house—on the walls, sitting on tables, in cases, everywhere. Ok, new message: "Hey, so I've tried being loving and caring but you're not being fair so if you don't come over in the next 20 minutes, I'm going to chop your cousins' f****ing heads off and I'm serious. Love you, bye!" I had to hit replay just to make sure I heard what I thought I heard. And yep, I heard right the first time.

I was laughing now; this broad was tripping. Let me call her. It went to voicemail. I tried her again, and it went to voicemail again. *Dang it, Angela! Answer the phone.* Man, what is Baby T doing over there anyway? Shoot, I forgot to tell her about this morning. Ugh. I threw on some tennis shoes and ran out of the house and jumped in the car.

Angela's house was less than five minutes away. I pulled out of my driveway and my phone rang. I quickly answered, "Man, listen."

The voice replied, "What's wrong with you?" Ugh, it was Anna. *Dang it, man, not now,* I thought to myself.

I replied, "Nothing, just thought you were someone else." What was she even doing up? It was like 2:30 in the morning. She asked what I was doing. I said, "Nothing, going to pick my cousin up," which was not a lie.

She started talking again. "Oh hey, I've been thinking." (*Don't you say it…*) "I want to see you." *Dang it!*

I responded, "Oh, for real? Ok."

She started to say, "So when?" as I pulled into Angela's driveway.

I cannot make this stuff up; this crazy girl was standing in the doorway in a silk robe holding one of her samurai swords. Man! She was so fine but this broad was crazy. *Don't get distracted from the mission: Get Baby T and Nina get out; don't die.* "Hey Anna, I'm going to have to call you back in a minute." I got out of the car and walked up to the house as she walked out on to the porch. Oh, by the way did I forget to mention she lived next to a cemetery? Yeah, she lived next to a cemetery.

As soon as she stepped up to me as I walked on to the porch, she yelled, "Who the f*** are you talking to on the phone this late?

"Man Angela," I chuckled, "you better gone."

She snatched my phone out of my hand before I could even blink, looked at it and said, "Oh, you talking to this b**** again." She yelled, "Whelp, you won't be anymore!" and threw my phone like Tom Brady throwing a touchdown pass into the cemetery. Yep, you heard me right; she trick played that mug deep into the cemetery.

"What in the hell. Angela—what is wrong with you?"

"You aren't gon' be talking to nobody but me!"

"Angela, I am not in the mood for this." I pushed past her into the house.

I started calling for Baby T and Nina. She yelled, "No, first you're going to listen to me." I ignored her and started walking toward the kitchen. She jumped in front of the doorway of the kitchen with the sword. She yelled at me, "So it hasn't even been twenty-four hours and you're already talking to another chick?"

"Angela, I'm not doing this with you; you were in bed with a whole other person this morning. Move." I pushed past her.

"Jamihla, I love you," she said.

I yelled down the basement stairs, "Baby T, Nina, let's go. You should have loved me this morning." They ran up the stairs and I yelled for them to go get in the car.

"Jamihla," Angela yelled as they walked out to get in the car.

I turned around, getting annoyed, and yelled back at her, "WHAT! What could you possibly have to say?"

She started crying. I turned and walked out. Cry me a river.

I got in the car and pulled off; Baby T was like, "Me-Me what just happened?" I told them the whole story, starting from the morning, and they were dying laughing. Baby T said, "Hey man, she really is crazy!"

I laughed to myself and said, "Man, I know," thinking, *What in the hell did I get myself into?*

The next day I told my grandma I lost my phone and she got me another one. I was back in business before 4:00 PM. My contacts didn't transfer so when I got an unknown call, I answered it. "Hello."

"How in the hell did you get another phone already?" Yep, it was Angela!

I replied, "My grandma—what did you think was going to happen? You thought I would just go without a phone since you chucked it in the cemetery? Why are you calling it anyway, if you thought I didn't have one?

"I was trying to teach you a lesson. You're never going to learn anything if your grandmother keeps doing stuff like this," she replied.

"Man, bye Angela." This chick was really nuts, man. She called back again and I hit ignore but for some reason I didn't think this would be the last time she called.

CHAPTER 21

A couple of weeks went by and Angela continued to call. Sometimes I answered, sometimes I didn't, but every time she tried to get me to come over and I declined.

I started chilling with this chick Brandy, the cousin of one of the little chicks Baby T was cool with. Baby T and I were over at her house a lot but the only problem was that she was married and her husband thought we were just over there to chill with her cousin. I know, I know what you're thinking. Yes, I am a piece of crap and I fully acknowledge that. This was so wrong. This was someone's wife, and even though the dude was a total dick, it was still wrong. But I wanted what I wanted and clearly, I was not the best decision maker then.

Anyway, her husband thought that when we were over there it was for her little cousin. Brandy and her cousin were super close so it was only natural that we would all be together. One day we were all chilling and the cousin was like, "Why don't you guys just stay here since it's so late." If I had used the sense God gave me, I would have said no. But God left the building a long time ago so I said, "All right."

As we went to bed Brandy was upstairs with her husband. This "made sense." He had to leave for work around 5:30-6:00 AM, I believe. Baby T, Brandy's cousin and I fell asleep downstairs. I was on the couch knocked out when I awoke suddenly as something slid under the covers. It was Brandy! My heart was beating 1,000 times a minute "What are you doing?" I asked her. She started kissing me. "What if he comes down here?"

"He's asleep," she said. *Oh my God, I'm going to die,* I was thinking, but we couldn't stop. About ten minutes later I heard a creak. If you've ever been doing something you weren't supposed to, you know that sound. That noise was the pressure of someone's foot being applied on a floor board. I almost had a heart attack because I knew it could only be one person, her husband. I pushed her to get off me and she jumped up. I turned over and pretended to be dead—not asleep but dead. I was literally not breathing. I had no idea what she was saying to this dude but I had to get the hell out of there. I heard them walk into where we were at and I was still not breathing, and after a few seconds they walked out. I waited until I heard them in the distance before I breathed again. *What in the hell is wrong with you?* I thought to myself.

Morning came; Baby T and I went home and got dressed and came back, and I told Brandy that I was only staying until 'Oh boy' got off work and then I was out. We were watching TV while Brandy was in the kitchen cooking, Angela had been calling my phone since yesterday but I did not answer, especially since I was over here.

It was a great afternoon. My phone had stopped ringing. I was still alive and the chicken Brandy was cooking smelled delicious. Then out of nowhere Brandy yelled, "Oh hell no! Jamihla, you better get this girl before I beat her a**."

I was confused. "What are you talking about?"

She was looking out the window and she said, "Angela." I walked over and looked out the window and this broad was in this woman's driveway. Who told her where I was and how in the hell did she find me? Why was she just sitting there? Brandy said, "You better get her."

"All right, all right," I replied. It was pouring rain. Ugh, this darn girl, man.

I ran outside and I could hear Ray J's "One Wish" playing from her car as soon as I stepped out the door. I hopped in her car and asked her, "Angela, what are you doing here?"

"I missed you and wanted to make sure you were ok."

"How the hell did you know—you know what? Never mind. I'm fine."

She asked, "Are you hungry?"

"No."

"Do you need a ride home?"

"What? No. Angela, you can't be here."

She asked, "What is it about her?"

"Angela, I'm just chilling. That girl is married and you and I are nothing. Look, I gotta go; you need to leave. I'll call you later."

"Do you promise?"

I rolled my eyes, "Yeah, I promise." As I stepped out of the car, she turned Ray J all the way back up—ugh! Around 4PM Brandy dropped me off at home. I was not doing anything today; I needed a break.

A few weeks later my friend Hillary and I were chilling. It was about 7:00 PM and we decided to split an X pill just for the hell of it. We were sitting playing cards at her dining room table and my phone started ringing; it was Angela. I ignored it and she continued to call until I had like eight new voicemails. Hillary was dying because Angela was blowing my phone up. I was used to it, because when she got on a roll Angela didn't stop. One thing about this woman: you had to admire her persistence. Hillary and I were so high that we kept laughing at everything and she convinced me to play the voicemails that Angela left. I knew they were going to be crazy because they always were when I refused to answer the phone.

New message received 7:46 pm: Hey, it's me; call me back when you get this. New message received 7:52 pm: Hey, don't know why you're not answering; call me back. New message 7:55 pm: Jamihla, I really need to talk to you; ok, bye. New message 8:00 pm: Here you go with this crap again. Stop ignoring my calls and call me back. New message 8:10 pm: Why aren't you answering the phone? New message 8:15pm: You know what? I don't know why I even bother; you're such an a**hole. Call me back.

Hillary and I were on the floor dying laughing; man, what was wrong with her? New message 8:20 pm: Hey, I was wondering if you were hungry. Let me know; bye.

Ha, ha, ha! I was laughing so hard I was about to pee on myself. New message 8:30 pm: Hey, I just wanted to let you know that I'm still here. I'm still loving, I'm still caring, and I'll be here whenever you're ready to talk. Ok bye, love you!

We were laughing so hard we were crying. Through heavy breathing from laughing Hillary was like, "You have to call her back, please, you have to call her back."

I was laughing so hard I couldn't catch my breath. "Ok, ok wait, wait we have to pull ourselves together." I tried to straighten up and cleared my throat. "All right, all right, I'm good." I told Hillary I was going to call her but she couldn't laugh. She said ok, trying not to laugh.

I picked up my phone; her missed call was still on the screen. I pressed send. "Oh my God, I can't do this." I choked back a laugh. "Hey, what's up?"

Angela replied, "I was wondering when you were going to call me back."

It was killing me not to laugh then. "Yeah, so what's up?"

"Well, I was wondering (Hillary had her hand over her mouth, holding back laughter) if you wanted to come over. I cooked and didn't know if you ate yet or not."

Hillary was mouthing, "Yes, say yes, say yes, please, we have to go."

I told her ok, I would be over there in a minute. She responded, "Ok, I'll be waiting."

I hung up.

CHAPTER 22

We were back on the floor dying with laughter. I didn't know if it was funny because we were so high or funny because she was crazy. We got into the car and headed out to Angela's. I looked at Hillary. "You know she's going to be pissed when she sees you." We started laughing again. We finally pulled up to her house and it looked kind of dark. I knocked on the door. Hillary was standing behind me to the side, trying not to laugh.

Angela opened the door with a huge smile on her face. She had on a robe that was slightly opened and looking behind her, I saw candles lit everywhere. She said, "Hey" and stepped out of the way for me to come in.

I stepped in the door and Hillary popped over like, "What up doe, what you got to drink?" I was dying laughing on the inside.

When she saw Hillary, her face changed and I could tell she was pissed. She said, "Hurry up and get in, letting all these bugs in."

"Man, why you got all these candles lit?" I asked her. She was walking toward the kitchen, and I went into the bathroom. The whole tub was lined with candles. For some reason I couldn't stop laughing. I asked her, "What did you think was going to happen tonight?"

Angela said, "I didn't know you were going to have Hillary with you. I thought it was just going to be me and you."

Hillary said, "Dang, I'm hungry too. I like to eat."

This was pure comedy. Part of me felt bad and then the other part of me was like, "Naw, I don't love these hoes." I could tell

Angela was upset so I told her I was going to drop Hillary off and come back.

She said, "If you leave, you're not going to come back."

I told her, "Yes, I am."

I left and dropped Hillary off after we had a good laugh. I headed back to Angela's. It was almost midnight as I was driving up Main Street. My phone started ringing. It was Brandy. I answered, "Hey, what's up? Where are you?"

"I'm out; meet me at your house."

"All right, I'm down the street," I responded. I loved it when she did that. I didn't know if it was the thrill of sneaking around or that she never really questioned what I was up to. She was always telling me that she was ready and I needed to get there.

I pulled up and she was already there. I hopped out of my car and into her SUV, and you already know what happened next. Sorry Angela. This became Brandy's and my thing. She called and said she was out or I'd shoot her a text in code telling her to get out, and it didn't matter the time of day or night. It could be 11:00 AM at the park or 3:00 AM at the crib; it was whenever, wherever. She was the only one I made an exception to my rule for, and I had so much fun with her. The next day Angela asked what happened to me and I told her I got sick and had to go lie down. I told her that I would come through later but we both knew that probably wasn't going to happen. I know it may seem like I was hard on Angela but trust me, if I explained every single detail to you guys, it would take me a whole other book. I really didn't even know why she kept trying. Was she really in love or was it just hard for her to hear 'no?' Either way, I was off on my next adventure.

A few weeks later, I was talking to one of my dudes who came down from Toledo to DJ on the weekends. Whenever he was in town you knew it was going to be live. Anyhow, he was down here and had a couple of his friends with him and one of his home girl's saw me and asked him for my number. We had been talking since then and she was coming down this weekend. I was probably just going to lie low and chill until she got here, unless Brandy called. Ok, pop quiz time for those of you who have been paying attention thus far.

Do you remember that little voice that used to torture me my entire childhood up until about nine or ten months ago? Have you heard it lately? I haven't either. See, that's exactly how the enemy works! When I was torn, broken, and didn't know which way was up, he kept pushing and pushing me, until I reached who I had now become—someone who didn't care about anything; someone who did whatever they wanted, whenever they wanted, and didn't care about the consequences or anybody's feelings. I was so void of actual feelings that my sense of humor became morbid.

One day I was sitting in the car with Aubrey and I pulled a gun out and put it to my head. It wasn't loaded but I just wanted to freak her out. I thought it would be funny. It was only when she started crying hysterically that I was like, "Oh shoot, maybe I went a little too far. Why would she think I would kill myself?" I was just joking. I never even realized how much I probably traumatized her. This was the type of stuff I was doing, and there was a complete disconnect between right and wrong.

There was no need to push me anymore. I was gone; he had me. Now all he was doing was cheering on my narcissism and reckless behavior and giving me everything I thought I wanted. And this is why we haven't heard that voice in so long.

CHAPTER 23

This particular weekend I was going out with my homie Shawna and her cousin. We met at her cousin's house and we had a few drinks before we went out. Whenever we were together it was nothing but laughs. Shawna brought up the time Anna tried to run me over and we were cracking up. Her cousin asked in all honesty, "What do you be doing to these girls that makes them so crazy?"

And I gave him the same answer I always gave. "Nothing, they do it to themselves."

We got to the club around 11:00 PM and I met up with my girl from Toledo. We were sitting in a booth and I couldn't even remember how much I had to drink, but I thought I was seeing things when I saw Brandy walk through the door. I had to be tripping. *What is she doing here? She doesn't even go out like that.* She was looking around and I knew she was looking for me. She knew this was where I hung out. I slid down a little in the booth and as I was getting up, I told Toledo I would be back.

Brandy was walking through the entryway to the other room as I walked toward her from behind. When she turned around to come back toward the bar, she saw me and looked me dead in my eyes. I smiled but she had this pissed-off look on her face. She walked up and discreetly whispered, "Let me holla at you in my car," and she headed outside.

I followed her to the car, got in, and asked her, "What's up?"

"I heard you were here hugged up with some chick."

"What? Naw, they must have me mixed up with someone

else."

She looked at me and said, "I know you; who is she?"

"There is no chick. Besides, what are you doing here? You didn't tell me you were coming out tonight. Ain't ol' boy at home?"

"Don't worry about how I'm out; I know you up to something."

I leaned over and kissed her neck. "No, I'm not!" I was lying through my teeth and she knew it.

"Ok, you said there's no chick, there's no chick. Come on then, let's go have a drink."

I replied, "Come on," as cool as a cucumber, but I was wondering how in the hell was this not going to blow up in my face.

We walked through the door and over to the bar and I ordered two drinks. It was a good thing I had some loyal friends. I gave Shawna a quick rundown on what was going on and she informed Toledo that I was in the middle of a situation but I would link up with her later at Shawna's cousin's house. I saw Toledo nod and look at me, and I watched as she got up and began walking in my direction. I started sweating bullets at this point. I was trying to size the situation up in my head. Best case, she just keeps walking. My heart is pounding. Worst case, she says something to me and Brandy flips out later because she's not the type to cause a scene, especially since she had a man at home. I felt my heart beat in my throat. Toledo was about fifteen feet away from me and still walking.

I hit the bar. "Ay, let me get another shot," I said hoarsely.

Brandy looked over at me. "What's wrong with you?"

"Nothing," I said, my voice cracking. I felt like my heart was going to pop out of my chest. Why was I so nervous? I was single! Toledo was right here and she looked at me, smiled and winked, and kept walking.

Thank God, I thought, as Brandy said, "What are you staring at?"

I shook my head and said, "Nothing" and downed another shot.

The bar was coming to a close and Brandy asked what was I about to do. I told her that I was going with Shawna and the others to her cousin's house and then home. She told me that she would meet me at my house in about an hour and I said, "Ok."

Now this is the part where things get a little hazy because I was wasted. My night ended with Brandy finding out about Toledo, taking my keys and chasing me around my car, while I was trying not to be killed, as Shawna and her cousin were standing in front of his place, laughing uncontrollably. Yep, I think that just about summed it up.

I called Toledo the next day to meet with her at the hotel and apologized for the messed-up night. She was cool about it and said that after being around me, she would be crazy to think there weren't other women. We hung out and talked for a while and made plans for me to go out and see her in Toledo. I left thinking, *Man, you have to slow down.* I finally talked to Brandy and she was pissed but it didn't last long, and we were back to our normal routine.

About a month after the Toledo incident I was at home in my bed. I rolled over from a good night's sleep. I picked my phone up to see the time. It was 10:00 in the morning. "Man, I must have been tired." I saw that I had five missed calls and a new voicemail. I didn't recognize the number so I played the voicemail first. When I heard the message time, I was thinking who in the hell was calling me that early. New message 6:58 AM: Ay, nigga when I find out who the f*** you are I'M TAKING YO MUTHAF***** HEAD OFF. YOU WANNA MESS WITH MINE; I'M GON' KILL YOU NIGGA. End of new messages.

Well, that escalated quickly. I picked up my phone, found the number I was looking for and pressed send.

"Hello."

"Hey," I said into the phone.

"Hey what's up?"

"Your husband called me."

"Oh my God, what did he say?"

"Nothing much; he just left a voicemail saying he was gonna chop my head off."

"Oh my God! What! Did he? How did he—?"

"I don't know," I interrupted, "but I'm positive he thinks I'm a dude. I'm gonna call him back though."

"And say what?"

"That I don't know what he's talking about and don't be leaving crazy messages on my phone. Matter of fact, I'm going to call him on three-way so you can hear."

"Ugh, ok," she replied.

I clicked over and scrolled to the number he called me from and called it back. He answered so I clicked back over so Brandy could be on the call. "Hey man, you call me?"

He yelled, "OH HELL NAW, YOU A B****?"

I was trying not to laugh at the ridiculousness of his question. "If by b**** you mean a woman, then yeah, man."

"Oh, hell naw. Nope, nope, she knows better; Brandy knows better than some s*** like this."

I cut in. "Aye man, you need to calm down; I don't know what you think."

He cut me off. "I pulled her phone records and saw how much y'all talk."

"So, when is it a crime to talk to somebody?"

He yelled, "At three and four in the morning?"

"Look dude, all that proves is I'm up late."

He said, "Y'all can be together; she knows better than this s***, man."

"Dude listen, that's your wife. I don't want her. You need to talk to her because it sounds like y'all got some problems. Don't be calling leaving no b.s. on my voicemail again." I hung up.

I called Brandy back. "Man, you better get this old nigga together before I have somebody tune him up."

Brandy responded, "Ugh, all right man, let me call him."

I lay back down in bed. "Damn it man, why this old dude gotta be so insecure?" I mean, technically he had every reason to be, but still…

Ok, so let's recap right now. I'm on my whole 'I don't love these hoes' thing (just messing with chicks for fun; nothing serious). Anna, I was really feeling but she messed that up and kind of messed me up. My friend, that wasn't really love or anything because we already had love for each other from being friends for so long. So, I don't think she really even counted. Anna was really the reason my motto was "I don't love these hoes." Angela was just, well, I don't even think it can be put into words. But I really, really loved what Brandy and I had—no strings attached. We both had our own lives and when we met up it was all about us, and it was amazing. And now this old dude knew. Ugh, I hated to even think about it but I knew Brandy and I were going to have to end it. "Damn it, man!"

As you can see, I was a complete narcissist! At this point somebody's marriage was in jeopardy and I was mad about a hook-up. Brandy and I met up a few more times but old boy was paranoid as hell now, and it was getting harder and harder for her to dip out like she used to. We ended with nothing but love and I told her to let me know if she ever left the dude.

CHAPTER 24

Time moved on. In my city they have this event called 'dollar night.' You can get a shot of whatever liquor you want for a certain period of time for just $1.00. Tonight, we would be going to dollar night at Ol' Skool. This was the one place that we went that sometimes I would have trouble getting into. There was this one bouncer who knew my mom and knew I was underage so he wouldn't let me in. We got there and he was not at the door. Yes! That meant I would be able to get in. We would probably stay for a few hours and then go around the corner to my friend's bar. Don't forget, all my friends were older than me.

We ordered like ten shots apiece so we didn't have to go back up to the bar. We lined the shots up on the table in front of us and I felt a tap on my shoulder. I looked up and man, it was this dude, the one I was telling you about earlier. He looked at me and said, "You already know."

"Ugh, all right, man!"

He said, "Go ahead and finish your drink really quick and then you gotta go."

All right, now this may have been one of the dumbest things I'd ever done, and remember, I'd made some pretty poor decisions thus far. I'd already had one shot and one of my friends tossed me the keys to her car and said, "Just take my car and we'll meet you at the next spot."

I said, "Cool" and I downed nine shots and finished my beer. Yep, you heard me correctly! I downed nine shots of vodka back to back and chased it with a beer before I jumped in the car to drive to another bar.

I arrived at the next spot and walked in. Now, for those of you who don't know the effects of alcohol, let me tell you something. Sometimes when you drink you don't feel it immediately. It could be a few minutes before it hits you; it could be an hour. And it takes one shot approximately one hour to clear your system. So, I had ten shots total in less than fifteen minutes. Can anybody guess how messed up I was going to be eventually?

Ok, where were we? So, I walked in and I was feeling fine and everybody was like, "Ay, yo, what up, Jamihla?"

I nodded. "What up? The bartender asked if I wanted my usual and I said, "Yeah." She walked away and came back with a shot of Grey Goose and a Bud Light to chase it with. I downed the shot and took a sip of my beer. Count em up; that's eleven shots plus one beer. She brought me another shot as I was talking with the owner's sister. Somebody was having a little get-together and we decided we were going to go, but first I decided to go get my grandmother's SUV because it had more room. Why I needed more room for two people I don't know, but at the time it seemed like a good idea.

I figured my friend could get her car back since I planned on going somewhere else and then I would go home after. I downed my shot and finished my beer off. Are you still counting? That's twelve shots plus two beers in less than one hour. Was I drunk yet? I didn't feel drunk. I was not stumbling or slurring my words, was I? Clearly my decision making was impaired, because I got in the car and drove under the influence to go get another car.

Side note: I know my story may be interesting and downright comical at certain points but I'm telling a cautionary tale. Please don't drink or do drugs and if you do, which I truly hope you won't, please don't drive. So, where was I? Ah yes, so I was driving clear to the other side of town to pick the SUV up. My friend's sister was with me because she was going to follow me and drive my other friend's car back. The music was blasting and we were feeling it on the trip out there. We arrived at our destination.

I hopped out of the car and jumped in my grandma's SUV. I pulled out of the driveway and as I was driving down the street, I felt around in the compartment on the driver's side door for one of my mixed CDs. I pulled one out and popped it into the CD player. I turned left onto Lexington Avenue. Now at this point I knew the liquor was kicking in because I felt invincible and I didn't realize how fast I was driving. The music came on and it was one of my cuts. The chick on Busta Rhymes' song came through the speakers. "Touch it, bring it, pay it, watch it, turn it, leave it, stop, format it, touch it, bring it, pay it, stop it, turn it, leave it, stop, format it." And as the song played, I turned it up even more as the beat dropped.

I was driving faster and faster, not realizing I hit 80 mph in a 35-mph speed zone. The light before you get to Main Street turned yellow and I knew it was going to turn red before I could make it through. I looked down and saw how fast I was going, and I was at 85 mph! There was no way I could stop or slow down in time. I blew the light, because if I tried to turn and go with the curve of the road, I was going to flip the SUV.

If you've ever had a moment when you knew your time was up and you were about to die, then you know what I mean when I say everything slowed down and came into focus. I knew there was nothing I could do to change what was about to happen and I was at peace with it. I knew I was going to die. I know that sounds crazy but even through the drunkenness I knew it was out of my control. I caused it so I had to accept it for what it was. I knew my fate was to burn and I had accepted that a long time ago.

There was a Papa John's on the corner of South Main Street with a tall sign that stood out in front of the store, and it had four yellow cement pillars around it. I waited for it to be over as I lost control of the vehicle. I hit one of the yellow pillars at full speed and it didn't budge. The airbag exploded simultaneously and it was lights out.

When I came around, I was in the hospital. The nurse who was taking care of me told me I was in an accident. She said that I hit a pole going about 100 mph and I was lucky to be alive. She said, "You must be really popular because our lobby was so packed with people concerned about you that we had to call the police department to control the crowd." I figured people may have poured out of the bars and come to the hospital.

From various family members and friends, I found out the scene of the accident was so bad that everybody thought I was dead. The ones who made it to the scene before the ambulance took me away said they knew I would be ok because I was yelling at the medics to get off me. Sorry guys. I heard my mother was so distraught she could barely walk. Sorry I put you through that, Mom. I also heard I acted a fool when they brought me in because I didn't want to wear the neck brace. They said I was so intoxicated I swore up and down that I wasn't driving. I heard I pleaded with my aunt to take the neck brace off and when she wouldn't I turned into the little demon from *The Exorcist*. They had to put me in restraints and somehow, I got out of them. And I guess I negotiated with them and they let my PNC come in, in exchange for me calming down.

My grandmother was happy I was alive and wanted to strangle me at the same time. Out of everything I'd done so far, disappointing her had to be the absolute worst feeling in the world. She showed me a picture of the scene of the accident and the car. The whole front of the car was gone; you would have never even thought it existed in the first place. The engine was sitting in the front seat, protruding into the backseat.

A bystander who lived across the street from Papa John's heard the noise from the crash and ran out to see the SUV mangled and smoking. He said it was smoking so bad that he thought it was going to catch on fire. He ran over to see if he could see anybody and he found me in the fetal position under where the glove compartment used to be and pulled me out and called 911. Thank you, sir, for saving my life! He told my grandmother there was a reason I lived and that God must have one heck of a plan for my life.

After all the scans came back, I had a small fracture to a bone in my back that would heal on its own, a pierced lung that they weren't really too concerned about, and bruised ribs. Other than that, I was fine—not one scratch was found on me. The doctor told me I would be sore for a couple of weeks and then I would be able to resume normal activities. Everybody kept telling me how lucky I was; I received a lot of flowers and 'get well' cards. People stopped by to check on me and see if I was ok. My friend Sade stopped by and had me laughing so hard I thought I was actually going to pop a lung; she was always good for a good laugh. My baby brother was there to help nurse me back to health with his multiple trips to get me stuff that I couldn't get myself. I couldn't make it all the way up to my room so I had to commandeer my little cousin Sharell's room until I could make it up and down the stairs with ease.

After a few weeks I was all healed up and back to my old self. When people saw me for the first time after the accident some were emotional and some told me how scared they were, and how glad they were that I was ok. I didn't drink for a while but after a few months I was back to partying again, full force.

CHAPTER 25

I ended up having to go to court for the accident and was charged with an OVI (operating a vehicle under the influence), Reckless Operation of a vehicle, underage drinking, and I'm sure there was something I'm forgetting. The judge threw the book at me; he could not have cared less that I almost died. He was out to teach me a lesson.

I had to go to jail for five days and I was placed on probation for one year. My driver's license was suspended for six months. I had to have a mandatory alcohol assessment and 40 hours of AA meetings. I also paid restitution and over $1,000 in fines and court costs. I was pissed and in my irrational little mind I thought I had every right to be. I didn't hurt anyone but myself, my grandmother had insurance, and the Papa John's pole was still standing, ugh. Ok, let's recap again.

As a child, even though everything seemed great on the outside I had a lot of internal struggles. Traumatic events warped my view of myself and of God. I'd accepted my fate and that I was going to hell and I'd decided to live for myself and do whatever I wanted. I'd grown accustomed to juggling multiple women and I was borderline narcissistic. I'd almost killed myself drinking and driving and I was back drinking already. The judge just threw the book at me and I was pissed. I think that about covers it.

When I turned myself in to do my five days, I was on the work release program. So, my grandmother picked me up from jail, drove me to work, and brought me back when I got off at 10:00 PM. On the first day, after I went to work and came back, I found a note on my bunk. When I opened it, I saw it was from one of the other females in the dorm stating how she liked me and wanted to get to know me better. I was pissed and disgusted. Now, I may mess with women on the outside but to me you have to really be gay to mess with someone in jail and I just wasn't there, crazy hun. This was the most disgusting place I had ever been in in my entire life. The last thing on my mind was getting to know anybody.

I threw the letter in the trash as the girl watched, and she hopped up off her bunk and started screaming, "You just gon' disrespect me like that." Oh, and did I forget to mention she was the first person in Mansfield that I heard of that had contracted the AIDS virus?

I looked at her and said, "Man, you better..." and before I could get anything else out this girl, Tricia, that I knew from high school hopped off her bunk and said, "B****, you better sit down and the next person that writes her a letter I'm going to shove it down their throat." I never got a chance to thank her for that. Then she walked over to me and gave me dap and said, "Don't worry about them. I got you; you don't belong in here." Once my five days were up, I was so thankful. I went home and took a long hot bath.

A few weeks later my grandmother and I had a talk. She wanted me to move into her other house with my other cousin's baby mom. My cousin Montay used to live there (her old house that we grew up in). She already had spoken with the baby mom's father and they were supposed to split all the bills with me. I agreed to do it; besides, she was the mother of my favorite little guy.

At this point I was eighteen years old. I had gained quite the reputation for myself with women. I loved partying and I was moving out into the world as an adult. I worked a full-time job at a glass factory and the work was easy, but I hated doing the same repetitive things every day. A lot of the old heads loved me because I always made it fun at work. This led to me being 'talked to' sometimes by our supervisor Janet; however, it was never anything serious. Besides Janet knew I didn't care about anything she had to say.

My cousin's baby mom and I lived together and things were going ok. I loved seeing my little cousin every day and his little smile would light up the world. He was walking now and trying to say his first words. He would always look through the handle part of the sliding door to my room and start speaking gibberish to wake me up in the morning. Man, I miss those days!

This particular weekend was just like any other weekend. I didn't have to work, so I was meeting up with my friends at Alexis' house and we were all going out. As always, we were out and were having a good time. I was buzzed and once I had a few drinks in me, as we know, I was liable to say anything.

From across the room I saw this chick (the blonde bombshell) and I asked one of my friends who she was and, they give me a quick little rundown on her. Her name was Jessica and she had two sons and she used to talk to this lame guy I'd heard of.

I walked over to her and said, "What's up?"

She said "Hey Jamihla."

Oh! She knew my name. We talked for a few minutes about nothing and before I walked away, I snatched her phone and put my number in it and said, "I'll see you at my house later on tonight."

She looked at me, shocked, and then started cracking up like, "Man, you're crazy; bye Jamihla."

I said, "We'll see" and walked off, chuckling to myself.

Now at this point in my life I had realized how powerful my words were. I could get almost any woman to do anything I wanted. The spirit of lust was on me so heavy that all I had to do was plant a seed in a female's mind and they would eventually call me because of their curiosity. Men either hated me or loved me, and some thought I presented a challenge to them since it seemed like

I only liked women—key word here: seemed. I remember one time I was out with my friends and we were dancing when one of my stepdad's friends came over and tried to start dancing with me. Ew. He then proceeded to tell me how he would give me $2,000 if he could watch me with another woman. He then tried to kiss me. I tried to smack the black off this dude I was so disgusted. He just laughed and said his offer still stood.

Anyway, where was I? Later that night we were all back at Alexis', still kicking it, and my phone rang. It was about 3:30 in the morning. I didn't recognize the number. "Hello."

"Hey what you doing?"

"Who is this?"

"Oh, you give your number to so many girls you don't know who's calling you?"

"Naw, it just took me a minute to catch your voice. What's up?"

"You busy right now?" And just like that. I knew I had her.

"Naw, just chilling."

"You wanna go for a ride?" she asked.

"Why not? You need the address?"

"I'm already outside."

I smirked and told my friends that I would holla at them the next day and they were cracking up because they heard my exchange with the blonde bombshell earlier that night so they already knew what was about to happen.

I hopped in the car and we talked for a while and then we rode to my house. My roommate was gone for the weekend. I asked the Blonde Bombshell if she wanted to come in and she said yeah. We went inside and we talked and laughed. She was laughing and said she had never had anyone be as direct with her as I was. She didn't even like women, so why would I approach her like that? I told her it wasn't because of some vibe I picked up from her. If I saw something I wanted, I would go and get it. "What's the worst that could happen? You tell me to get the hell out of your face!"

I was leaned up against the counter top and she was looking at me in a kind of disbelief. We were only a few feet apart and she asked, "So what did you mean when you said you were going to see me tonight?" as she was walking closer.

I said, "I can show you better than I can tell you" and I grabbed her and kissed her. I picked her up and sat her on top of the counter and showed her what I meant. She ended up leaving later that morning, after sleeping for a while, and I got dressed and met up with my friends.

They asked what I got into last night and I told them we just talked and they started laughing and saying, "Yeah, right! You would not just spend time talking to anybody after midnight."

I laughed. "Whatever!" I knew everything they were saying was true.

CHAPTER 26

I had an AA meeting to attend. I hated these things but I needed to get my paperwork signed to show my probation officer I was compliant with what the judge told me to do. We were in this day room sitting in a circle and I just wanted to get out of there. People were telling stories of how they had lost their wife/husband and kids because of their drinking and I was thinking I was not as bad as those people. I did not have a drinking problem. (I didn't have a drink every night but the amount I drank and the poor decisions I made when I did drink were a problem. It's funny how we can convince ourselves that we are fine because we are not as bad as the next person.)

This lady was going on and on about how she sneaked and drank the mouthwash because of the alcohol content in it and I was thinking, *What in the hell—how do people get this bad?* I was not where they were and just listening to that depressing crap was making me want a drink. (See what I did there? I was in AA and I was so annoyed I was thinking about how I couldn't wait to have a drink! But remember, I didn't have a problem.)

I got my paper signed and I was out, off to another week of work and then the weekend to party and repeat all over again. The blonde bombshell and I were talking more and becoming really good friends with benefits. She was cool and down to earth and no signs of crazy had popped up yet. Speaking of crazy, Angela still called every now and then, but I thought she was finally moving on.

The weekend came again and as usual we went out. For me

not liking repetitive things, this sure seemed repetitive, don't you think? I had my little cousin Sharese's car so I decided to leave the bar around 1:00 am. I went home and lay down and around 3:30-4:00 AM my phone started ringing. I answered and tried to turn on my lamp and realized the power was out. I looked outside and none of the street lights were on. On the other end of the phone, one of my friends was telling me that Hillary just got into an accident and that she hit a pole by the 76 station. "Damn it, man!" I said ok and hung up, jumped up and got dressed.

The 76 station was around the corner from where I lived so I jumped in the car, praying she was ok, and headed around there. I was driving and I saw the 76 station but I didn't see the accident so I kept driving. As I was passing the 76 station, on the next street I saw a bunch of police cars with their lights flashing and realized the accident was over there. There were so many emergency vehicles I was scared of what might have happened.

There were railroad tracks right next to the 76 station and the bars weren't down and I didn't see or hear anything coming. So I pulled on them to turn around really quick so I could get to the scene of the accident. As I turned around and headed back the other way towards the accident, I heard sirens and saw the lights flashing. Damn it, it was the police. I pulled over and he walked up to the window so I rolled it down.

He asked for license and registration. I said, "My license was suspended." He asked me to step out the car. I got out and he asked why I was driving down the railroad tracks. "I wasn't. I was turning around; my friend is the one in the accident over there." I pointed past the 76 station. "I was trying to see if she was ok."

In a real condescending tone, he asked, "So why are you on this side and not over there?"

I rolled my eyes. "Clearly, I thought it was on this side and once I saw it wasn't, I turned around to go back." He asked why I was driving without a license and at this point I was starting to get pissed. Have I mentioned my short temper yet? "Did you not hear anything I just said to you?" I replied. He told me to calm down, which pissed me off even more because I was not yelling at him or anything. I was just answering his dumb questions. "I am calm; you're not listening."

"Ma'am, have you been drinking tonight?"

"Yeah, earlier; not lately." Then I realized. *Damn it, he can probably still smell it.* I only slept a few hours and hopped straight from the bed into my clothes and into the car. He thought I was drunk.

He asked me to take a breathalyzer and I refused. I told him that I acknowledged I was wrong and I would accept my consequences but could he just find out if my friend was ok. He told me that was none of his concern and for me to turn around so he could cuff me. At this point I lost it, and as he handcuffed me I began to yell, "You can't even tell me if my friend is alive or dead?" followed by calling him everything under the sun but a child of God.

I was already going to jail so I had nothing to lose at this point. As he was driving, I was fuming and the silence was killing me. Being the smart ass that I was, I said, "Hey Porky, could you at least turn on the sirens or something?" He told me to shut the hell up and I told him to shut the hell up. Have I mentioned how much I hate the police, especially MPD? And this wasn't just some bandwagon hate; this was from the things I had seen.

So, before any of you Blue Lives Matter people get offended, this is my story and what I saw through my eyes, and through my eyes the police were the enemy. When I was still in high school, I was hanging out with a bunch of friends at one of our friend's house. The police came and asked what we were doing there and our friend said it was his house and told them we were just hanging out. The police started asking for our names and one of our friends asked them, "Why? We didn't do anything wrong." And this jackass of a cop got pissed because she questioned him and grabbed her by her braids and said, "Because I said so" as he slammed her face first into the grass. Chaos erupted as her little sister tried to get him off her and I watched as two other officers ran over and tackled her and started beating her sister. It was one of the most horrific things I had ever seen.

When we used to hang out at McDonald's after the football and basketball games the police always harassed the black kids. When we would be at the park in the summertime, they always blew down on people, harassing people that weren't doing anything but hanging out. I watched them handcuff my cousin behind his back and then start yelling, "Stop resisting" as he was handcuffed and walking with them; then they started punching him. I watched my aunt try to protect her son from them beating him and then the police slammed her on the ground. I watched people call the police for actual help and they didn't show up for an hour.

There were only two exceptions to how I felt about our police department and those were Officer Toby and Officer Cindy from the DARE program. When they saw us outside of school, they still treated us like humans; other than that, it was, "F*** the police." I had no respect for the police whatsoever and I feared nothing and no one but God, even though I knew I was no longer a child of His. And all my frustration with the police from over the years was being taken out on this one cop.

I cussed him out until we got to the station and I was given to another cop for booking. Oh, did I mention when we got to the station, as I was still cussing him out, I looked over and saw Hillary through the glass? Thank God she was ok. I yelled her name and this chump was acting like she didn't know me. What the hell! I wouldn't even be here if I hadn't gotten up to make sure she wasn't dead. Whatever man! I'm here now.

They booked me in and I heard the officer I was cussing out

the entire time say, "That's Joan Day's granddaughter."
  I yelled, "And? Man, just take me to my cell."

CHAPTER 27

I was put in the cell with a bunch of other women. I grabbed a seat and chilled because I knew I would not be there long. Even though Hillary just acted like she didn't know me I knew she saw me, so it was just a matter of time before I would be bailed out. And just like I said, a few hours later, I heard my name called and I was told I was being released.

When I got outside Hillary was waiting in our other friend's car and she was cracking up. She said, "Man, you know I wasn't going to leave you in there but you were tripping last night." Turned out she hit a pole and she wasn't hurt but it knocked out all the power on the north end of town.

I started laughing, "That's why the lights wouldn't come on."

She asked what they charged me with and I told her, "An OVI, driving on a suspended license, and disorderly conduct."

OK, let me interject for a minute: Nothing I did was ok and I was so rebellious and so stupid that I didn't even care or know the ramifications of getting two OVIs (operating vehicle under the influence of drugs or alcohol) in less than a year. People, please don't be like me.

A couple of weeks passed and I was standing in front of the same judge. He peered down over his glasses at me. "Weren't you just in here a few months ago for this very same thing?"

I thought, *No dummy, a few months ago I was drunk and got into a car accident. This time I was drinking earlier in the night. I was not drunk when I went to sleep, nor was I when I woke up. But I did have alcohol in my system. Then I was given the wrong information and had to turn around when I was pulled over by one of your douche bag cops, and now here we are, Judge!* But I simply replied, "Yeah." I didn't say "yes or your honor" because I didn't like the dude and I had no respect for this justice system. So I felt like this was a way for me to rebel by not addressing him appropriately. He doubled what he gave me the last time and I didn't expect anything different. I did my couple of days in jail and was back out and back to my normal life.

I would be turning nineteen that year and Hillary and I decided we were going to have a party. Her birthday was ten days before mine. One of the local places people went out at would allow you to throw parties for free if they knew enough time in advance. You just had to pay for anything else extra you wanted. There was a dude, KD, known for throwing parties so I reached out to him and he set everything up and also did the fliers. I had to give him props, as he had these fliers all over the city. The party was about two weeks out and my mom was well, let's say a little upset about it. She asked me if I thought it was wise to have a party in an establishment that sold liquor when I was underage and on probation for alcohol-related offenses. No, it was not wise but I did what I wanted and that wasn't going to change now. So, I just told her that I would be all right and not to worry. I knew she wasn't happy but what could she do? I was grown now.

Over the next week I worked so much overtime that by the time day five of six came, I was exhausted. When I lay down to bed that night I was out, which was unusual for me because I had become accustomed to running off about four or five hours of sleep. I had a dream that night that I was standing in my great-grandmother's front yard (the one we called Gramma). I heard her call my name and when I looked up, she was right in front of me (she'd been dead for about eight years). I could feel this warmth, like I was wrapped in her arms, even though she wasn't touching me. The sky was blue and the sun was shining and you could hear the birds chirping. She looked at me and smiled and said, "Jamihla, be careful who you give your heart to because once it's gone..." The ground started shaking. I looked up the street, which was uphill, and I could see the roads cracking and the foundations of the houses splitting. The ground was moving under my feet and I could see Gramma falling. I reached out to try to grab her as she said, "It's gone" and collapsed in front of me. I screamed, "GRAMMA." I looked down and I saw my heart beating on the ground. I could not breathe; I was gasping for air. I woke up and I literally could not catch my breath.

I rolled out of bed on my hands and knees onto the floor, and I was still crying like I was in my dream as I was trying to suck in air. It took me a minute to realize where I was. When I finally got my bearings, I sat with my back against the bed thinking, *What the heck just happened?* as I realized I was at home. *Super weird.*

The day of the party came and I couldn't wait to kick it. All my friends met at my house for the pre-party. My friend Kelly brought over his sound system and there were more bottles than I could count. I was wearing crisp jeans that were dark blue and faded to a lighter blue with a black-button up with white pinstripes. I had a white with white pinstripes suit jacket on over my button-up and a pair of all white mid-Air Force Ones. You couldn't tell me anything!

When we arrived at the venue, we lined up outside the side door, which was usually locked but was now used as an entrance. You could hear the music thumping from outside. My friend Amanda was in town from school and she was part of our little entourage. She went inside to let the DJ, who was also the party planner, know that we were outside.

After a few minutes I heard the music stop. KD said, "I want everybody to get up and wish Jamihla and Hillary a happy birthday."

As the door opened Rick Ross's song "Hustlin" came on. "Every day I'm hustlin', every day I'm hustlin'…"The fog machine went off and you could barely see as we walked in. As we walked on to the dance floor, I had my pimp goblet in my hand and Amanda popped a bottle of Moët and poured it into my cup.

The bartenders brought out bottles of Moët and put them on the tables that were designated for my friends. I drank out of my cup and handed it off as the song switched and the introduction to Crime Mob's "Knuck if you Buck" came, on which was my cut. The beat dropped and my friends and I went crazy; everybody—and I mean everybody—was instantly up and feeding off our energy. Everybody was jumping around, and this place went from 10 to 100 in a split second.

We were having so much fun that I forgot the blonde bombshell was supposed to meet me there and walk in with me. She was calling my phone over and over again but I didn't get it because my phone was in my pocket. I realized the room was packed but I didn't realize that it was past capacity and the blonde bombshell could not get in.

The rest of the night was a blur and when I woke up the next day I was stretched out across the bed on my stomach with all my clothes still on except my suit jacket. I felt my phone stabbing my leg. I pulled it out of my pocket; my battery icon was red and I saw all the missed calls and texts from the blonde bombshell. Damn! How did I forget about her? Oh well, she should have been on time. I knew she was pissed so I didn't bother calling her yet. I looked at the clock and it was 1:18 in the afternoon. I sat on the side of the bed blinking while grabbing my head. Ah, my head was pounding. What happened?

The last thing I remembered was dancing with some chick from Cleveland and the rest was a blur. I saw my white suit jacket on the floor in the corner of the room. There was something red all over the front of it. What happened? I walked over to examine it and realized somebody must have bumped into me with a drink or something, because it smelled like alcohol.

CHAPTER 28

I got myself together and popped some Tylenol and called up my PNC to have her take me to Church's to get something to eat to soak up all of this alcohol in my system. Man, I felt like crap! We went over to Alexis' house and the usual's were there. Everybody looked like they kicked it way too hard last night so we all decided to just chill and lay around and watched movies.

On top of all my extracurricular activities with these women, I started talking to this guy I used to go to school with named Keith. Keith was used strictly for sex. Whenever I wanted to be with a guy, I called him and within a few minutes he would be pulling up in his Suburban. It wasn't like he was a secret or anything. Some of my friends knew about him but he served only one purpose. We would talk sometimes but it was the way you would talk to your friends and he had no problem with 'our no strings attached' policy.

A few months later my friends and I were kicking it and I got sick. I hadn't even had that much to drink but I couldn't stop throwing up. I went home and the next day I smelled food cooking and I got sick again. What was wrong with me? I looked under the sink for some mouthwash and I saw the entire pack of pads.

I sat on the floor with my back against the wall and realized I had not seen my period and as I stopped to really think about it, I had missed it for the past couple months. I panicked as I replayed events in my mind of how this could be possible. I remembered the time I was with Keith and the condom broke and we didn't stop. I threw up again, thinking what this could mean.

I made a doctor's appointment but I could not be seen for another week. I took a pregnancy test and it was positive. This could not be right. I took another one: positive. I told my PNC and two of my other friends and they actually got excited and started making all these plans. I was petrified. I told them that I didn't want them telling anybody, not even Keith.

On the night before my appointment my stomach started cramping really bad and I was thinking *yes* because I always had horrible cramps with my period. Maybe those were false positives. I went to the bathroom and realized I was bleeding—yes, my period. I lay down and decided to still go to my appointment the next day. What could it hurt?

My PNC drove me to my appointment and I took another test and did an ultrasound. The doctor came in and informed me that I was having a miscarriage. I began to cry because I didn't understand. This couldn't be right; it was just my period. I was not pregnant; I couldn't be pregnant. I mean I couldn't have been pregnant.

The doctor was explaining how this happened and I was young and it would be ok. He said from the looks of things I would not need a D & C but he wanted to do a follow-up. My mind was just gone. I felt completely empty sitting there thinking about everything I did to contribute to this—the smoking, the drinking, the pills. I didn't know; I had no idea I was pregnant. What in the hell was wrong with me; how did I miss this?

I felt 1,000 pounds of guilt and I felt like along with all my other sins, I could add murderer to the list. I pray one day you can forgive me, sweet baby. I told Keith everything and he was saddened at the fact and more supportive than I could have ever imagined. I swore my friends to secrecy, and I buried this way down deep and locked it in the box with all the other things that I wanted to forget and covered it up with alcohol.

CHAPTER 29

A few months went by. I was with Hillary at the liquor store when I saw this tall blonde getting out of a Mercedes Benz SUV. I must have been staring because Hillary said, "You can forget about that one; you ain't pulling her."

Oh ye of little faith, I thought as I asked who the blonde was. She told me that her name was Janice and that she was with this lame dude. I was like, "Oh yeah, I've heard of him, but I've never seen her before." *I am going to find a way to talk to her—just watch,* I thought to myself.

We went in and grabbed a bottle and met back up with our friend Jill, who was bringing along Megan, this girl from her job. Megan was super sweet; she had just graduated high school not too long ago and seemed like she had no business hanging around us. There was a kind of innocence to her, and she took to me like a moth to a flame.

Over the next few months she became my little homie. We spent a lot of time together just hanging out. One of our favorite things to do was watch *American Idol.* Sometimes we would fall asleep together but that was the extent of it. For some reason, she was kind of precious to me and I didn't want to ruin her. She would ask me about the other girls she saw me talk to and I would keep it limited to what I would tell her. I didn't want to spark too much curiosity in her because I knew how dangerous that could be.

One night we all were kicking it and Hillary said that this dude James was having a party at his house so we all decided to go. We were having a good time when the chick that I saw a few weeks ago, Janice—her dude interrupted our conversation. He was going on and on about what he had and I looked outside and noticed he was in her car. I'd had a few drinks so all filters were gone. At this point he was getting on my nerves. So, I asked him, "How you acting like you ballin' and you driving your girl's car?" It seemed like after I said that everything stopped and everybody tuned in to what happened next.

An argument erupted between us and ended with me telling him how lame he was and that I was going to take his chick. Yep, you heard me: I told this man I was going to take his girl and I meant every word of it. Of course, he was pissed and said that it would be a cold day in hell before a dyke pulled his girl. I really hated that word dyke; it didn't really make sense to me, but I was going to show little buddy better than I could tell him. His cold day in hell was coming sooner than he knew.

A year went by and I kept seeing this chick Janice from time to time but never at a place or time when I could talk to her. I heard that she was not with old dude anymore—shocker—but she was talking to somebody who was friends with one of my friends. Dang it, I just needed one chance to talk her and that was it! Preferably after I'd had a few drinks; it seemed like alcohol gave me some type of seducing superpower.

I was still hanging with my little Megan almost every day. I went to work and came home and would have a drink if I was not out with my friends. Megan would come over when she got out of class or off work and do her homework. She was going to school to become a nurse. I really developed a genuine love for her and I knew she had a crush on me. But the way I was, I knew I would do nothing but hurt her so I refused to cross that line. I also became friends with this chick Gina. She was friends with Janice, and it was all a part of my plan to get closer to her. I found out she worked night shift, which presented a little challenge but nothing

I wasn't up for. Gina and I hung out sometimes in hopes that I would run into Janice but it didn't happen.

Months went by and it was like we were two passing ships. Gina would tell me she came as soon as I left, or I would get somewhere and she left right before I got there. This was the longest game of cat and mouse I had ever played and I had no intentions of giving up, and she had no idea that she was even the prey.

I had so many hookups with chicks in this time span that I had lost count. I had even hooked up with the ex-boyfriend of one of the chicks I was messing with. I was completely out of control and had no plans on stopping.

I didn't have time to invest in actually chilling with chicks for too long. I was on a mission. Megan was the only one besides my friends I spent time with but like I said, I wasn't crossing the line with her. I was almost two years into this pursuit of Janice when I was starting to lose hope. My phone rang and it was Gina. She was out with Janice and they were going to be at a house party. *Yeah baby*, I thought to myself. *This is it!*

I called Megan and asked her if she wanted to go to this party. She said yes, so I got dressed and waited for her to get to my house. We headed out to the party and I must say Megan actually looked really good tonight. We got there and went in about an hour and a half after I talked to Gina. I was saying, 'what's up' to people as I looked around for Gina but I didn't see her. I went into the other room and grabbed a drink for Megan and me. I texted Gina, "Where are you?" She texted back. They had left already; Janice had to go and change her shirt. Ugh! What the hell, man? I went and gave Megan her drink and tried to forget about my thoughts of meeting Janice.

Megan and I were enjoying our drinks and talking. About forty-five minutes later my phone vibrated. It was Gina. She said there was an after-hours party and wanted to know if we wanted to come over to Janice's and have a few drinks before it started. We could all ride together from there. *Cha-ching*—this was the moment I had been waiting for, for almost two freaking years. The chance to have one conversation with this woman. That was all I needed, just one chance! I was confident in that fact.

I got the address and Megan and I left and headed over to Janice's house. While we were pulling up to the house Megan told me that there was something she wanted to talk to me about. I asked her if she wanted to talk now or if she wanted to wait until later. She smiled and said that later was fine. We got out and walked up to the door, I knocked and Gina answered. We exchanged 'what's ups' (greetings) and proceeded into the kitchen.

Janice was in there with a huge bottle of Grey Goose and she was pouring drinks. She said, "Hey Jamihla." Yes, she knew my name. I said hello. She asked how I would like my drink. I told her straight and if she had a beer or something to chase it with, that would be great. I introduced Megan and we all sat down at the table, talking and drinking. I had no idea when I was going to get a chance to talk to her alone, but I was not messing up this opportunity.

We all got into her Benz and she put the panoramic sunroof back (this was the span of the entire roof of her car, and it was amazing). We got to the after-hours and it was packed; music was playing, food was being cooked and everyone was there. I had been over here multiple times before. This wasn't the first after-hours they had and I was friends with the lady of the house's son. After a few hours the party was winding down and everybody was leaving. I had been talking to Janice for most of the night but still didn't have her where I wanted her as yet.

I went upstairs to use the restroom and when I came out, she was up there. She said that the lady of the house asked her to grab something out of her room for her and would I happen to know where it was since I'd been over here before. I pointed to what she was talking about on the dresser and she grabbed it and turned around and said, "Why are you looking at me like that?"

I was all out of ideas. I felt like I had two seconds left in the fourth quarter and there was nothing else to do but go for it. What was the worst that could happen? Would she smack me? I grabbed her by her waist and pulled her into me with ease; man, she was so tall. I grabbed her by her neck and I kissed her without saying anything. I just kissed her. I felt her legs go weak and she fell back on the bed. She stood back up and she said, "Oh my God" and kissed me again. She said, "We can't do this here; we can't do this here" and I agreed and we walked back downstairs. We played cards for a little and then we all headed back to her place.

Once there, we all had another drink before the night came to an end and she walked over to me and asked if I wanted to stay. In my head I was screaming, *YES, YES, YES!* But I just said 'sure' nonchalantly and walked Megan outside to her car. Megan asked why I was not getting in and I told her I was going to stay a little longer. She asked me why and I said, "To talk to Janice," and I felt like I was seeing her heart break right before my eyes. Part of me actually felt bad about it because I loved her but I also loved her enough to know I was no good for her. She pulled out of the driveway with tires screeching, and I knew she was mad at me.

I walked back into the house and Janice was sitting at the table with her legs crossed. I felt like I had waited an entire lifetime for this. She grabbed my hand and led me upstairs to her bedroom. She shut and locked the door, and after that nothing was ever the same.

CHAPTER 30

The next morning, I woke up and Janice was not in there so I figured she must be downstairs. I put my clothes on and straightened myself up and prepared to go downstairs. I opened the door and in the bedroom doorway directly across the hall I saw someone I went to high school with standing there eating a bowl of Ramen noodles. They said, "Hi, Jamihla." I was mortified! I slammed the door shut and put my back up against it as if that would make them disappear.

What was she doing here? Wait, wait…I replayed the events of the night in my mind. She had four daughters, but I thought they were little. Wait—she talked about seeing me play basketball but I just thought she meant she saw a few games. The realization washed over me as I pieced together the drunken conversation.

I realized I had just slept with someone's mom. *What is wrong with you, Jamihla?* I thought to myself. Whelp, it was too late now; what was done was done. I opened the door back up and she laughed. I said, "Hey" and in the most awkward way ever I asked, "So is Janice your mom?" She said, "Yep" as she continued to eat her food. And then she said that her mom was downstairs.

I headed downstairs thinking this was crazy—even for me, this was crazy. I got downstairs to the kitchen and there were some people sitting there and Janice was cooking and asking me if I was hungry. I said, "Sure" and I noticed one of the people was the dude she was supposedly talking to. Once again, I had allowed my lust to get me into an awkward situation. I ate the plate of food she made for me and man, could she cook! She took me home and we talked in the car.

I told her that I didn't know I knew her daughter and she laughed and said that she told me last night. I told her that I didn't ever remember seeing her at our games and she said she looked way different back then. I asked her about the dude that was at her house that morning and she said that they were never serious; they just talked and she was really good friends with his mom. She said she called him over to tell him that nothing would ever come of it because after last night she wanted to see where this went. I said, "Oh really?" and she said, "Yes, or am I one of your little one-night stands? I've heard about you."

I told her, "No, it definitely wasn't a one-night stand." She had no idea how long I had been waiting to meet her. She put her number in my phone and told me that she had to work the night shift but wanted to see me in the morning if I was available. I said ok and called her so she would have my number saved in her phone. She said that she would call me on her way to work and I got out of the car.

I went upstairs to my room, lay on my bed, and started kicking and screaming. "YES, YES, YES!" I was on cloud nine. I hopped in the shower and afterwards just lay on the couch. I didn't want to do anything except wait for her to call. We talked her entire drive to work, which was over an hour away, but it seemed like we had only been talking for ten minutes. And this is what we did on her drives to and from work. If she wasn't at work or with her kids, she was either with me or on the phone with me.

After a few weeks I met her kids, and I had gotten over the fact that I knew one of them from school. I cut off all the other people I was talking to or messing with, and it was kind of like I was caught up in this whirlwind. I thought I had everything I had ever wanted so I finally came out to my mom and told her I was dating a woman. Not like she didn't already suspect it, but we had never had a conversation about it. She told me she loved me no matter what I did but I knew deep down it bothered her. I introduced her to Janice, and my grandmother seemed to like her. My grandmother also didn't have any warnings like the one that came when she met Angela.

A few months later my grandmother was diagnosed with lung cancer. She was the strongest woman I knew and cancer didn't stop her. She would do her treatments and still go to work. I never knew how she did it but after a while a part of me felt like she was getting tired, if you know what I mean.

Eventually Janice and I moved in together and I couldn't have asked for more. She bought me anything I wanted; she would cook anything I wanted, anytime I wanted it, and she never complained. She got to know my friends and they all loved her. Things were going great and she ended up proposing to me a little before we hit the one-year mark, and of course I said yes.

CHAPTER 31

We took a trip to Cleveland to go hang out with some of her friends from work and have a few drinks. On the way home, I fell asleep (I was on the passenger side) and woke up to red and blue lights flashing behind us. While an officer was talking to Janice, another female officer came over and asked me for my information. Now why do you need my information when I'm on the passenger side sleeping? I hate the police. But I gave it to her and there were two warrants for my arrest, for failure to appear. Ugh!

So, a little before I met Janice, I got in trouble again for driving under suspended license and some other stuff. I went to court but refused to go and see my PO. I was so tired of dealing with those people downtown that I just stopped going. Not the wisest thing to do but hey, that's what I did. The officer asked me to step out of the car and I did, and she cuffed me and put me in her car. Might I add what a douche she was, and I was actually being compliant with her.

She drove me to meet a Mansfield cop at a halfway point so he could take me into custody. I started to get nauseous in the back of the car and asked her if she could pull over so I could throw up. "No, and if you throw up in my car, I'm charging your a**!"

"You're going to charge me with puking?" Ok, GI Jane. I wished I could meet her out of uniform then we would see how tough she was.

We got to the meeting point and the cop from Mansfield took custody of me. When we got into the car he asked if I was ok and I told him, "Yeah."

He said, "Troopers can be real dicks."

I said, "Tell me about it." He asked what my warrant was for and I told him. He said that sucked and I should make sure I got it taken care of because I looked too young to be caught up in the system. I said ok and thought to myself, *Wow, this cop is acting like a decent human being.* He asked if I wanted a cigarette because it would be a while before I got the chance to smoke another one. I said yes, and we sat there and smoked before we began my journey back to jail. I was in there for two weeks before the attorney Janice hired could get me out.

On the day of my release I had to go before the judge before I could get out. He told me how all of my decisions kept leading me here and he was scared that if I didn't change, I was going to end up in prison or dead. He told me that I had three months to get a job or he was putting me in jail for six months.

My cousin's father was a supervisor at a youth detention center and he helped me get a job there. Oh, the irony! The job was cool. I was working on a unit with girls who had behavior issues. For the first couple weeks they tried me, until they realized I was not a punk and they were not going to do whatever they wanted. After I had to put a few of them in restraints they gave me their respect.

It was actually cool talking to kids about not going down the wrong path because the Lord knows I knew how rough it was. As I looked at them, I honestly didn't want them to make all the mistakes that I had made. I became cool with a few of my co-workers and almost every night after work we either went back to my house and drank and played rock band or went out and had a drink. Janice was usually either waiting for us or at work.

It was a Tuesday night and Janice was off, so we decided to go to the bar to get a drink. We walked in and my favorite bartender was there. She smiled and poured us our usual as soon as she saw us coming through the door. There was only like three other people in there besides us.

Janice and I were sitting at the bar laughing and drinking when the door burst open and a guy ran in, moving so fast that he knocked me off my bar stool and landed on top of me. Another man ran in chasing him and I heard the gun shots going off: *pop; pop, pop.* My ears were ringing. I could feel the heat from the bullet slide across my cheek, and the guy who knocked me over got hit. He got up on his feet and ran into the bathroom as the guy was still chasing and shooting at him. I grabbed Janice and the bartender and threw them behind the bar and lay on top of Janice. The shooter burst back out of the bathroom and ran outside the door. After a few minutes, when it felt like it was safe to move, we ran out to the car and took off. The realization that I almost got shot in the face sank in and I was freaking out.

It was about 2:00 AM when I got to my mom's house and knocked on the door until she answered. I told her what just happened. I don't think she had ever seen me this scared, and I just stood there and cried as she held me in her arms.

CHAPTER 32

I was on my job for about a year and our squad on our unit was solid. Nothing went down when we were there and all of our girls respected us; even the kids on the other units respected us. I was starting to feel like sort of a hypocrite though, telling them not to drink and do drugs and as soon as I left, I knew that was exactly what I was going to do.

There would be mornings when I was still hungover from the night before. I would still go into work. That was usually when we would have movie day. We would bring in snacks and just have the kids chill in the day room all day and watch the latest movies that came out.

Man, something was really wrong with me. Remember when I told you I had everything I thought I ever wanted and technically I did? A nice SUV, somebody who gave me anything I wanted, a different outfit with Jordan's and the fitted hat to match for every day of the year, jewelry dripping from everywhere—I mean I really couldn't have asked for more. But that little lust demon was not satisfied and soon it was looking for the next thing it could devour.

I had started talking to one of my coworkers on another unit and we soon began talking about more than just work. I didn't know what was wrong with me. I knew I wasn't going to leave my relationship. I guess at this point I was just seeing if I still had it. And I did; this chick was hooked. We talked and texted all the time when Janice was at work but it hadn't gone beyond that yet.

I was moved to a different unit under a new lead because there was an opening. A few months after I was on that unit the lead and I started talking, but I wasted no time sleeping with her and that same rush that I used to get back in the day was back. I knew I was wrong but I literally couldn't stop myself.

The one that I hadn't slept with was probably worse than the one I had already started sleeping with because she was catching feelings. I mean strong feelings, and I was in too deep to back out now. In the midst of juggling these two women at work a new nurse started and we always would talk when I took the kids to med pass. This led to us exchanging numbers and yep, you guessed it: I ended up sleeping with her. She would do anything just to spend ten minutes with me. She was getting hotels just so I would stop by for thirty minutes to an hour to hook up and then be out.

I was a monster and it was like the more I got, the more I wanted. I honestly felt like something had completely taken over and I had no idea how to stop it. Somebody said something to Janice while we were at a concert about the one, I had not even slept with and she went off, demanding to see my phone. I was furious, honestly, not because she was asking to see my phone but because somebody was hating.

I stepped out of the concert and she followed me, yelling, "Don't try to delete anything off your phone now."

I said, "Whatever man, just take it; there's nothing to delete." I had made a habit of wiping my phone clean and turning my ringer off whenever I was at home.

She was scrolling through my phone and you could see the fumes coming off her. I was confident because I knew nothing was in there and then I heard, "What the f**** is this?" My heart dropped. What could she have found? Then she turned the phone around and it was a picture of me.

I was confused. I was like, "What? That's me."

She responded, "I know it's you, smart a**. Why did you send it to this b****?"

Dang it! I forgot to delete the picture I sent to coworker # 1 that she asked me for. I had become so good at this stuff with women I didn't even get angry. I just said, "You tripping; she wanted a picture for my number in her phone, nothing more and nothing less. If it was something I wanted to hide I would have deleted it, don't you think?" She threw my phone at me and was still pissed but she had not found proof of anything and technically, I didn't lie to her. I was not sleeping with coworker #1.

It took a few weeks for Janice to believe me and leave it alone. I told coworker # 1 that we had to chill, as it was getting too hot. Now that would have been fine if coworker #1 hadn't already fallen for me. She could not care less how hot it was; she wanted me, and that was that. She had me so shaken that I thought she was going to pop up at my house one day. The stuff she was saying to me was just crazy; I was literally scared of this chick.

One-night Janice and I and our other friends were out and we were having a good time when coworker #1 walked through the door. *Are you freaking kidding me? She doesn't even hang out in these types of places.* She was staring at me like she wanted to kill me with her eyes. I turned back around to the bar and I must have been tense because Janice was like, "What's wrong with you?"

I said, "Nothing." My phone started vibrating. It was coworker #1 and I saw it was a text but before I could check it to see what it said, more texts were coming through, all from her, so I silenced my phone.

I told Janice that I would be right back, as I had to use the restroom. I went in the bathroom and pulled out my phone. She was sending me every text message we had exchanged since the beginning. What in the hell was wrong with this chick? Granted, I did lead her on, but she knew I had a fiancé.

I had not even slept with her and she was acting this crazy. How did she even have every text message? What did she do? Save them? *Think, think, think.* I turned my phone off and sent one of my friends who could be a little intimidating to tell her to stop the b.s. before she had to put her hands on her.

I ordered a bunch of cans of beer from the bar because it was too late to purchase alcohol anywhere else. I told Janice we were going to go kick it at home. She went to the bathroom while I was waiting for the beer, and I told her to meet me in the car.

I was walking to the car with my arms full of beer and I felt this hard slap in the back of my head and all the beer hit the ground. It was Janice. "Is this why we're leaving, because your little girlfriend is here?" she yelled.

"That ain't my girlfriend and I didn't know she was going to be here; I can't stop her from going places," I responded. I picked up the beer and got into the car and yelled at her to get in the car. I started the engine and pulled off as I saw coworker #1 walk out of the bar.

A few weeks passed and I kind of had coworker # 1 under control. I still didn't let my guard down because I knew she was liable to do anything if I made her mad. The other two were good with how things were and never caused a problem. I convinced myself I needed to chill a little so I kept my extra activities to a minimum.

CHAPTER 33

A few months went by and everything was going smooth. We decided to head to Atlanta for my 21st birthday. A bunch of my friends went with us, and the trip was amazing. Every night had been a blast up until the last night of the trip.

They took me to a strip club. It was the actual day of my birthday and we were all sitting at the stage throwing money and enjoying ourselves when one of my friends brought over a stripper and said, "Jamihla, look." This chick looked like she could be the identical twin of an actress I was in love with back then, and they all knew it. The stripper asked if I would like a dance and before I could speak, Janice said, "Go ahead and take her in a private room."

The stripper grabbed my hand and took me to the VIP area. The room was rather amazing. She brought a bottle of Grey Goose in with her and we started talking as she started to take her clothes off. Ok, now Janice already knew what happened in those rooms but I thought she was giving me a pass because it was my birthday and because of who the stripper looked like. And besides, I was going back home with her at the end of the night. I truly believe everything would have been fine, if I had come back out of the private room before the club closed.

We've already established that something was truly wrong with me and when lust kicked in, I lost control of myself, ok? Like I said, I thought everything would have been fine but I was in the private room for three hours. Most people go in for ten to twenty minutes but nope, not me. I was in there for three hours. On top of that, all the money was in my pocket so Janice couldn't even buy a drink, and the security was so tight in that spot that they wouldn't let her back there. And just to take it up a notch, in true Jamihla fashion, as we came out the stripper tried to take me home with her. Yep, as if it couldn't get any worse, the stripper wanted to take me home with her. I don't think I need to explain how pissed Janice was and how she wanted to leave me in Atlanta at this point.

Moving on, Janice eventually forgave me. Life was progressing and going well, but of course that was not good enough for me. Janice was at work and a bunch of us were kicking it. Remember how I told you alcohol seems to bring a whole other beast out? Well, we were kicking it and I blacked out drunk and the next thing I remember was that Janice woke me up. I was in the neighbor's bed, by the way.

I do not even think the English language has words to describe how mad she was, and rightfully so. I was even shocked at myself. *What in the hell were you thinking? You are really getting sloppy, man. How do you get so drunk that you forget to go home and then get caught in someone else's bed? WHAT IS WRONG WITH YOU?* was all I could think to myself. I didn't even know how to begin to explain this one; I had no idea what I did last night. So, I just left, went over to one of my friend's house, and just lay there on the couch.

I didn't even know how I was going to come back from this. I called and talked to my neighbor and she told me that she went over and told Janice that nothing happened. I was over there and got so drunk I thought I was at home and passed out, and she just let me sleep. It was so dope of her to do that because I had no idea what to even say. I knew Janice would have to leave for work soon so I just stayed away the rest of the day and got my thoughts and myself together.

That night when I was finally together, I decided to take a trip to Janice's job, which was over an hour away. I got there close to the time for her to get off. She was supposed to get off at 3:00 AM that night, and when she walked out, I asked her to get into the car so we could talk. I apologized over and over again and told her that I had no idea what happened or how I ended up there. She was yelling at me and telling me how embarrassed and hurt she was, and I could not do anything but sit there and let her get everything out. I deserved every bit of it. She still loved me and wanted to be with me but she was broken right now and I didn't know how I was going to fix it.

We went home that morning and she finally fell asleep after crying, and I sat there and watched her sleep thinking, *What in the hell is wrong with you? How can you be this out of control?* I promised myself that I would cut everybody off and do everything I could to make her feel secure again.

CHAPTER 34

A year went by and I was on my best behavior and our bond was stronger than it had ever been. I got a call in the middle of the night that my grandmother had been rushed to the hospital. By the time I was dressed I got a call saying she was being taken by life flight to The Cleveland Clinic. Janice drove while my cousin Nolan and I sat in silence on the way to Cleveland. We got there and everyone was in the waiting room. I went back to ICU where the patient rooms were to see my grandmother. When I walked in, I saw that she had a couple of IVs hooked up to pumps and she was on a ventilator to assist her breathing. The doctor explained that the other doctors who claimed she was in remission were in fact wrong and that the cancer had spread. She seemed to be doing ok right now, and they were going to keep an eye on her.

After sitting around talking to family for a couple of hours we decided to go home and get some rest and come back later, since the doctor said she was doing ok. By the time we ate something and showered I received a call saying we had to get back to the hospital. We jumped back on the highway and by the time we got there I saw the dreaded expressions on everyone's faces.

They took us into a conference room, and I already knew what this meant. The doctor explained how she took a turn for the worse and there was nothing more they could do. The only way to keep her alive would be for her to remain on life support. And in that moment, if there was anything left of this damaged heart of mine, it had just left with the doctor's last words. My whole being was filled with emptiness and I knew that this was going to rock my family to its core.

I looked around the table at my aunts and at my mom. Some were crying; some were asking, "Are you sure there's nothing else you can do?" They went over our options and then left to give the family time to think. No one wanted to say it but after an uncomfortable silence I said it. "You guys know she wouldn't want to live like this." Everyone knew it was true. She was a woman of action; she was a doer; she was Joan freaking Day and we were getting ready to lose the matriarch of our family. After everyone agreed for the doctor to take her off the life support, we walked out to tell the rest of our family, and I was responsible for taking each one of my little cousins in to say goodbye.

As we were walking down the hall my mom's legs went out from under her and I caught her and tried to hold her up. People were breaking down crying. Before we even made it to the lobby, everyone out there already knew. I was a face of stone and I felt nothing but dead inside.

Once they said it was ok to come back, my mother and my aunts went and said their goodbyes. I walked my little cousins back one by one to say their goodbyes to not only their grandmother but their second mother. After everyone said goodbye, the whole family gathered in the hospital room and my uncle said a prayer. As my grandmother was taking her last breaths almost everyone left because they couldn't take watching it. But I stand there, partly because she didn't deserve to die alone and partly because I had to see it to know it was really happening. As I watched her take her final breath, I felt the last piece of me died and went with her.

CHAPTER 35

After the funeral and things died down one of my little cousins moved out of my grandmothers into her own place. Another one moved in with my aunt and it was decided that I would move into my grandmother's house and the other one would stay with me.

After we moved nothing about my lifestyle changed. It was like I partied even harder. People couldn't wait for the weekends when it was warm because they knew we were always going to have the grill going. I was even talking to my mom a lot more now, and she would come over often. I was still at my same job and I loved the actual job but there was a supervisor there that was really starting to work my last nerve. I managed not to get caught up with any woman, even though I felt like I was being tempted more now than I ever had been before.

Months went by, seasons came and went, but the partying had remained the same. Things with my supervisor hit their tipping point and I couldn't take the dude anymore so I quit. A short time later, I got a job in Columbus at another youth facility and it was always the same thing; the kids tried you until they saw you weren't soft, then they would calm down and give you your respect once they saw you in action.

My unit was filled with girls with conduct disorders and again I found myself with a solid crew. After a few months of working there we decided to move to Columbus. I would miss all my friends but I needed a fresh start. Janice took a new job so she could get off night shift and be home more with the kids. It was a big adjustment for her because she went from running an ER to working in an office.

I was happy she would be home at night now too, and that also meant way fewer chances for me to get into something. We always had fun at work and always found new stuff to do with the kids. The only rough thing about working with teenage girls is that some of them would tend to develop crushes and act out. I felt like I constantly found myself having to tell one of them, "You don't know what you like; be a kid."

Just like in Mansfield, my crew and I loved to drink, so that's what we would do when we got off or on the weekends. It was like same party, different city. After being here for about nine months the nurse on our unit quit and the nurse from the boys' unit was having to run back and forth to pass meds.

After a few weeks they hired a new nurse for our unit and we were introduced to Nurse Jazmyn. Jazmyn was about 5' 8", with smooth brown skin and shoulder-length black hair, and she always had a smile on her face. There was something about this girl I just could not put my finger on. Jazmyn seemed to be fitting in nicely with our unit. She didn't talk much, and it seemed like when she came on the unit she was in and out like she was always in a hurry to get somewhere. But no matter how fast she was moving, she always had a smile on her face. A couple of the kids had tried her already and she didn't put up with their crap, so I was sure she would be fine.

After a while she started having little conversations with us here and there, but she was usually in her office. You would always see some of the thirsty dudes from the boys' unit hanging around trying to talk to her. These dudes were pathetic, man. I think I may have forgotten to mention all these people slept around with each other there. Even if I was still on my creeping thing, I wouldn't have slept with any of these people. They all came off as kind of desperate, and there was nothing attractive about that. Anyhow, I think they probably had a bet on who was going to get Nurse Jazmyn.

I must say she was very intriguing; she didn't act like those other thirsty women around here. She carried herself different and sometimes I found myself wondering about her, not in an 'I want to sleep with you type of way' but in an 'I wonder what her life is like' type of way. I wondered why she was always smiling.

One day one of the girls on our unit started acting out and let's just say my anger got the best of me. This girl was a year shy of being grown (eighteen) and had a mouth that you could tell she had never been slapped in. Other staff members decided it was best that they dealt with the situation, and I was standing in our office behind a glass window.

She was running all over the place and they were trying to deescalate the situation. But that chick did not respond to talking. I knew they needed to grab her and just take her to the back. Whenever there's a situation on the unit the nurse has to be present. Someone opened the door to call Jazmyn out and this little girl picked something up and threw it through the door and knocked my hat off my head and I saw red. I took off to run out the door because I was sick of her. Jazmyn grabbed me and I fought to get out the door as she was holding onto me for dear life, trying to get me to calm down. She was finally able to get me to the other side of the office and told me to go out the other door and try to calm down. I walked out the door and I was pissed, more so because I allowed that little knucklehead to take me there (to that level). After ten minutes or so I went back inside.

I found Jazmyn and apologized to her. She showed me the bruise on her leg from me trying to get away and she looked up and smiled and said that it was ok. "I just didn't want you to lose your job over that kid." We talked for a minute and I realized how cool she was. After that incident Nurse Jazmyn hung out and talked more with us.

My birthday was coming up soon and we were having a little get-together, so I gave Jazmyn my number and told her to message me and I would send her the address if she could make it. The day of my birthday came and we were kicking it. Janice cooked all my favorite food and there was no way we would be able to get through all the liquor. Jazmyn texted me and said that something came up and she would not be able to make it. I messaged her thanks for letting me know and maybe next time.

Over the next few months Jazmyn and I talked more and I found out that she really was cool. Our conversations were not about meaningless crap; we talked about life goals. She asked me what I really wanted to do because she knew this wasn't it for me. I told her that I actually wanted to be a paramedic but I had not thought about that in forever. We both had aspirations to work with at-risk youth and we both also didn't think these kinds of places had put enough effort into actually helping these kids.

Man, she was different from other people I had talked to, and it was almost like I couldn't get enough of our conversations! Rumors started that there was something going on between us but there honestly wasn't. We were becoming friends and we loved each other's company. The thought of messing with her had never crossed my mind.

CHAPTER 36

Jazmyn and I took our lunch breaks together and started talking on the phone almost every day. One day she came in with information for an EMT program and asked me for some of my information and signed me up for classes. Can you believe that? There was someone who was so invested in seeing me grow that they took time to research it themselves! It was like I had no excuse but to do it.

She started coming over to hang out whenever everybody else would come over my house and we always had a good time. I remember the first time she met Janice. She was shocked and said, "I didn't picture your fiancé like that."

I asked her, "What did you picture?"

She replied, "Not that. This isn't it for you." I asked her what she meant by that and she just said, "I know this isn't it for you." I couldn't say I wanted anything from her; she was just a friend but she was different. I mean, everything about her was different and I knew it from the first moment I met her.

Dudes at work were still trying to get with her and when I asked her about it, she would say she just loved to flirt but would never mess with any of them. I explained to her how one had to be careful when doing stuff like that and there was a difference in dudes flirting and dudes talking to you like you're just another hoe. Trust me, I knew! There was something about this girl that made me want to be next to her but not with her. It was the most bizarre feeling in the world.

One morning I woke up with the worst pain on my right side

and thought my cramps decided to turn it up a notch this month. I felt sick to my stomach so I ran to the bathroom and threw up everything I had in me. I tried to sip water and that came back up. I couldn't keep anything down and the pain was becoming unbearable so I decided to call and tell Janice. When she heard my symptoms, she came home and said she thought I had a kidney stone and took me to the ER.

They admitted me to the hospital and doped me up and monitored me to see if I could pee it out. After scans came back, they realized it was too big so they scheduled surgery. They were going to use some kind of laser to remove it. When that didn't work, they had to go in and retrieve it. All of this took over a week and a half. I lost about twenty pounds. I was only eating a popsicle and a little container of applesauce a day, if I could keep it down. They had me so drugged up during that time that all I did was sleep.

The day of my surgery was the same day that we had tickets for a comedy show that we got prior to me getting sick. My surgery was in the morning and the show was at night, and I was determined to still make it. Janice, Jazmyn, and I had tickets and were going together. Everybody else flaked out. My surgery went fine and I lay down until it was time for the show. Jazmyn arrived and we got in my car to leave. She was surprised at how much weight I lost in the short time span and she was joking around with me from the backseat like we usually do while Janice was driving. I said something smart to her and she knocked my hat off my head. I started laughing but you could tell Janice was getting annoyed.

We got to the show and there was a little bit of a walk to get to the venue. The wind was blowing. Jazmyn had on these jeans with heeled boots, and a brown peacoat. Her hair was down today but she usually wore it in braids. The way the wind was hitting her took my breath away; it literally took my breath away. She looked like a model or something. And it still wasn't the feeling I got when I wanted to sleep with other women. I was just literally taken aback at her beauty.

I sat in between Janice and Jazmyn. The comedian was hilarious but Janice barely laughed, and I knew she liked this type of stuff. After the show we went back home and Jazmyn left. When we got into the house, I asked Janice what was wrong. She said, "That girl likes you; she flirted with you the entire night and right in front of me."

I said, "No, she doesn't. We're just cool. She doesn't even like women."

She yelled, "Jamihla, name one woman you've been with that liked women before they met you. You are everybody's exception!"

"She doesn't like me; we're just friends. You're overreacting."

She said, "Whatever" and stomped off to take a shower.

A few weeks passed. It seemed like Jazmyn and I were talking every free minute and we talked about everything. Some days we were on the phone for hours. We almost hated when we had to hang up. One day we were at work and one of the thirsty dudes that was always trying to talk to her said something crazy to her like he could see bending her over the counter. I got pissed when she told me. We kind of got into it—not an argument, but I just couldn't believe she would allow him to say something like that and not check him. I told her, "That isn't somebody that's trying to get with you because they want you. He wants to screw you, and coming at you like that is disrespectful if you've never given him a sign that's what you want."

We got to the hallway before the locked door leading to our unit and she said, "I don't understand why you're so mad. Do you like me or something?"

I looked at her and said, "I honestly don't know how I feel about you, but I know I don't like that."

(Side note: Women, don't let men talk to you like that; like you're nothing more than a sex object. I know how I treated women in the past myself and as I'm growing, I see how wrong I was. Hell, I knew how wrong I was then, but I was a piece of crap. Women deserve someone who sees the beauty in them, myself included. Never get tired of waiting on the one that is somewhere waiting on you and settle for a bum that wouldn't know a rose from a weed. Ladies, know your worth.)

Where was I? She was just looking at me with a questioning look on her face so I asked, "And if I did like you, would that scare you?"

She replied, "No" and I told her honestly, "I don't know how I feel" and I swiped myself through the door.

The rest of the day was spent thinking about why I cared how she allowed people to treat her. It was her life, but I knew deep down she was different. She deserved better than those little dusty dudes sleeping with everybody around here. Not necessarily me, but she was precious to somebody; I just didn't know who. There was something about this girl.

I started school and Jazmyn had classes too. Sometimes she would come and hang out with me before I went to class if I didn't work that day, or she would wait for me to call her when I was headed home from class. We were becoming best friends and, in some ways, I looked up to her.

We were still having our little get-togethers but I was drinking less. I would drink on the days we had people over but I wasn't partying as hard as I used to. It was really weighing on me that I was telling the kids at work one thing and doing another. Plus, working full time and going to school full time, I really didn't have time to.

Janice and I were starting to argue more and more. She still didn't care much for Jazmyn. She thought I was changing and she was upset that I wouldn't quit my job. I would tell her I appreciated the fact that I didn't have to work if I didn't want to but I genuinely liked my job. I knew for a fact that I didn't have to work if I didn't want to but I also knew she only wanted me to quit because Jazmyn was there.

CHAPTER 37

A short time later Janice was injured in a car accident at work and had to go through physical therapy. This was hard on her, not being able to do everything she used to. They gave her pain pills for the pain and on top of not slowing down with the drinking, I felt like it was just making her angrier and angrier. I did do a lot in the past to make her insecure but I hadn't done anything in years and my only focus now was going to work and school, which made for some seriously long days.

I was off Tuesdays and every other weekend. I would spend Tuesday doing homework all day before I had to go to class. But it seemed like every Tuesday something bad would happen; either the kids would start acting up or Janice and I would get into it about something. I would always find myself talking to Jazmyn about it, and we started calling them terrible Tuesdays because like clockwork, every Tuesday something terrible would happen. It got to the point where I thought about switching my days off. Jazmyn would tell me that my life was like a movie but she truly had no idea.

Every night I came home from class I was accused of being with Jazmyn. Janice would go on a nonstop rant, cussing me out and telling me everything I was doing with Jazmyn when all I did was go to class. I was so exhausted I wouldn't even argue with her anymore. I would just say ok and walk upstairs. I was at the point where I didn't know what to do anymore. There would be nights that I would have to call Janice's best friend over to deal with her because I was too tired.

I would go to work at 6:00 AM and was in class until 10:00 PM and then until almost 3:00 AM I would argue with Janice or try to get her to calm down. It got to where I threw all the alcohol away in the house, every drop. I didn't even want to drink anymore, and by the time I would come home Janice would be drunk. Part of me felt like I drove her to this and the other part of me knew there was nothing I could do to stop it. I would spend time searching the whole house for any stashed liquor to get rid of it. She even got clever to the point where she was hiding it in water bottles. I was watching my entire relationship fall apart, and this time I actually hadn't done anything.

I would talk to Jazmyn about everything going on and she actually would try to give me advice to try to make things better with Janice. But there was no making things better. I tried to invite some friends over to help take her mind off things, and I invited Jazmyn so she could see that there was nothing there. We were all having a good time and Janice got so drunk that she passed out. I tried to wake her up but she didn't budge. Jazmyn was admiring my pool table and said that she never learned how to play.

Everyone had left and it was just me, Jazmyn, and Janice passed out on the couch. I showed her how to hold the stick and then I handed it to her. I laughed as I watched her struggle to hit the ball. I told her to hold it like I showed her but she couldn't properly place her fingers for whatever reason. So, I showed her how to place her fingers and then I got behind her to show her how to hold the stick. As soon as we touched it was like being zapped with electricity. And in that moment, I knew. I knew every feeling I said wasn't there had just come to the surface, and she felt it too. And we just stood there and looked at each other for a second before I awkwardly said, "Yeah, that's how you hit the ball." The energy between us was so strong it felt like I was standing in a magnetic field. I tried to shake it off. We played a little more pool before I walked her out to her car and said goodnight.

When I got back in the house, I shut the door and just stood there thinking, *Damn it man, this is not happening.* We continued to talk and both acknowledged what we felt that night and how we felt for each other. But she knew I was with somebody and I would never cross that line because I had way too much respect for her. She was worth way more than being somebody's side chick. It was amazing that we still found things to talk about but we did and it got to the point where literally every free minute I had I was on the phone with her.

Janice got to the point where she gave me an ultimatum: her or Jazmyn. Since I wasn't sleeping with Jazmyn or anything like that, I flat-out told her to do what she wanted but I was not going to stop being friends with somebody because she didn't like them. Come to think of it, she made me think more about Jazmyn than Jazmyn actually made me think about Jazmyn.

From the time Jazmyn and I became friends, every day Janice would beat into my head that I was messing around with her, and I wasn't. I was not blaming her but I was at the point where I was tired of her bringing up Jazmyn's name. Janice saw that I was not budging so she remained pissed but she didn't leave me. Our relationship had become so splintered over the past six months that I didn't care what she did. I just wanted her to stop bothering me. Part of me wished I was cheating as much as she accused me.

A few months later I was taking a CPR class and Jazmyn and I were texting. She told me that she was going out to lunch with this little weirdo from our job that looked like Kirk Franklin. I was instantly annoyed and asked her, "Why would you go out to lunch with this dude, and you know he likes you?" She told me that she knew he liked her but she didn't like him; she was just going for the free meal. I was so irritated with her and this free meal crap.

When my class was over, she finally called and told me that

Kirk tried to kiss her. I was so mad I had to pull over because I was starting to see red. I started yelling at her, saying, "What did I tell you?" I wanted to kill this dude. Why was I so angry?

She was like, "I didn't let him. Why are you so mad?"

I was still yelling and I said, "Because I'm in love with you, obviously." I couldn't believe those words "in love" just left my mouth—what in the hell!

There was a long pause and she said, "I love you too."

And I knew I was screwed because I had no idea what I was going to do next.

CHAPTER 38

We still didn't act on anything and continued to talk. Easter was coming up and she invited me to church. I explained to her how I hated church and everything that went with it. She asked me to just come for her, and how could I turn that down? So the day came and I met her at her place. She introduced me to her sister and her son and we headed off to church.

When we pulled up, I realized it was a mega-church and I was already annoyed, but I said I would give it a chance so I did. Once we were inside everybody was trying to give me hugs and I just kept sticking my hand out because I didn't know these people. We walked in and found seats in a sea of people and after a while the lights dimmed and the spectacle began. I was sitting there thinking, *What in the hell is this?*

It was like a three-ring circus. There were way too many theatrics going on right then. The lights that reminded me of the club, somebody won a car, good faith miracles were happening if you sowed a seed, whatever that meant. I couldn't wait for it to be over. When we left and Jazmyn and I talked about it I said, "Yeah, I would never go back there. They seemed like a bunch of weirdoes and there was just way too much going on. She said she knew I would say that but it was not always like that. Would I please think about giving it another chance? I told her we would see but I had no intention of going back to Never-Neverland.

I went back home and when I walked through the door World War Three broke out. Janice was yelling at me. She couldn't believe that I went to church, and I was changing. Once I went to church,

I wouldn't be gay anymore. I looked at her and asked, "What in the hell does that even mean? I'm not gay now. I like what I like. How is that going to change?" She just kept saying watch, watch, and yelling that she couldn't believe that I went to church. I was so confused. "It was just church and I didn't like it anyway. Calm down."

A few weeks later I went to see Jazmyn. We ended up leaving my SUV at her friend's house since it was so recognizable. Like an idiot, in my cocky era I had "MY OWN COMPETITION" written on the back window. Anyway, we got into her car and went to her house and we just talked and I realized all the reasons I had fallen for her.

As time went on, with all the arguing and fighting, I realized I loved Janice but I was not in love with her. I knew that I was in love with Jazmyn and I had never felt like this about anybody. I meant a feeling that would make you risk everything and not care about the consequences. But I still would never cross that line without permission because over our time spent together, I found out who she was precious to, and it was God. No matter how many demons I struggled with, I had enough respect for Him to not do to her what I had done to others.

She finally convinced me to go back to church again, even though I still had my doubts. It wasn't as bad as before and the message was decent, but I was still skeptical. When I returned home, again it was nothing but fighting as usual, but I no longer cared. She started again with the church was going to change me and make me think that our relationship was wrong. But I guess I just never understood her, because from the time I was a child I knew these things were wrong in the sight of God. But God was not in the equation for me.

I left God a long time ago and I knew I was destined for hell. I didn't live the way I did because I wanted God to approve of it. I lived for myself and was at peace with my fate. That night she got drunk and asked me why I couldn't let this girl go. She said that I had been able to let everybody else go for her, so why not Jazmyn. I told her that I didn't know. She asked if I loved this girl and I told her the truth. There was no more lying in me. I said yes, and she broke down. I told her nothing had happened between us because I didn't want to lie to her, but I knew she didn't believe me.

One of my coworkers was having a get-together at one of the bowling alleys and Janice didn't want to go so I asked Jazmyn if she wanted to go. She said, "Sure" so I told her I would pick her up. When I arrived at her door and knocked, she opened it and the sight of her made me weak. She was wearing dark jeans, silver flats, and a red Guess sweater that fell off her shoulders, with big silver dangly earrings. There were so many things I wanted to say. My mind was racing. But I just smiled and said, "Hey, you ready to go?"

We got to the bowling alley; the coworker whose birthday it was had a slight crush on me and it annoyed the heck out of Jazmyn. But she was cordial because it was the coworker's birthday. Everybody was getting drunk while Jazmyn and I were just sitting there laughing at people.

When the night came to a close, we were all standing outside talking and the birthday girl was playing around and slipped and twisted her ankle. She started crying for me to help her up and I did. She was wasted and she told me that she rode with someone else and asked if I would take her home. I agreed to take her because she was so drunk. I couldn't leave her here like this. Jazmyn was pissed. This was the first time I had ever seen her mad. I helped the birthday girl off the ground as Jazmyn was yelling for her to get up. I helped her into the backseat of my car.

Since my coworker lived up by me, I dropped Jazmyn off first because she lived about twenty-five minutes in the opposite direction and it was already killer late. Looking at her, I could tell that she was still mad and it was kind of cute to see her like that.

We got to Jazmyn's house and I walked her in. She told me how annoyed she was with the birthday girl but I said that I had to help her. I told her that I would call her as soon as I dropped the birthday girl off and I gave her a hug. I pulled back to let go and she pulled me back into her and kissed me, and in that moment, I knew what all those girls felt when I kissed them. I was completely gone. Whatever sense I had left had just left the building and she took over whatever little piece of my heart that Janice had left. I was madly in love with this girl and I knew my relationship wasn't going to last.

Tuesday rolled around and it was the day of my practical's (hands-on test) for the EMT program. I was super nervous. I wanted to pass everything the first time; retesting was not an option. I tried to call Janice to see if she wanted to do lunch on her break but she didn't answer. That was kind of weird of her but it was ok. I tried to call her again, and again no answer. I was lying down and I heard the door downstairs slam closed. That was weird because Janice was at work and the kids were at school.

I got up and my room door burst open. It was Janice. "You liar, I hate you, I hate you. I'm done," she yelled.

I asked, "What are you talking about now?"

She threw a forty-page booklet with yellow and pink highlighted strips on it at me. I looked down at it and it was my phone logs for the past couple of months. She highlighted every call and text to and from Jazmyn and every call and text to and from her. She was yelling at me that she couldn't believe how much I talked to her and that I couldn't wait to be off the phone with her so I could call Jazmyn and talk to her for hours. She was yelling about a time we were on the phone for almost seven hours. Dang, what could I say? She was right. I did talk to her a lot. She kept going on about how she hated me and that she was done.

While she was yelling, I called my aunt, who lived about ten minutes away, and told her that I needed her to come and help me. I started packing all my clothes and then she was yelling, asking me what I was doing. I told her that she was done and I was done and was leaving.

My aunt arrived in what seemed like two minutes and I had all my clothes loaded in what seemed like less than fifteen minutes. Janice had stopped screaming. She looked like she was in shock that I was actually leaving, but I was.

CHAPTER 39

I called Jazmyn and told her everything and she was in utter disbelief. "She actually printed off all of your calls?"

"Yep."

She asked how I felt and I told her that I guessed I was ok. I really didn't know but I would call her after my test.

I got settled in the guest room at my aunt's and headed to school for my practical's. My instructor came over and asked if I was ok. I told him that I was ok. He said, "I've never seen you look so stressed out." I gave him a quick rundown of my last five hours before I came to class. He asked if I wanted to test the next day with the other class. I told him, "No, I am ready."

I went through all my testing stations feeling like I was there but I was not there. We got to the end and we were all sitting in the hallway against the wall as our names were called individually to hear our results. Some people were talking; I was just sitting there with my head in my knees, thinking about the events of the day. I had no idea what I was going to do next. It seemed like hours went by and I finally heard my name. "Ms. Young."

I went in and there were three judges sitting there. The older woman began to read back how I did on every station and she got to the end and said only one other student and I passed every station. "Congratulations!" I was so happy I smacked the table they were sitting at and shouted, "Yes!" and thanked each one of them. I walked out feeling like a weight had been lifted off me. I called Jazmyn, told her I passed, and then I went to my aunt's to finally lie down and breathe for a minute. After I talked to my aunt for a little, I took a shower and lay down and I just cried. I didn't even know why but I just cried and cried until I fell asleep.

The next morning, I could not move; I physically could not move. I felt paralyzed. I could not get my body out of the bed. I called in sick at my job and they told me to take all the time I needed. I just laid there numb inside; I didn't move or talk to anyone. Jazmyn called to check on me and I told her that I was ok and we would talk soon. For the next three days I just lay there, not moving at all. My aunt tried to get me to eat but I couldn't; I just lay there.

On the third day I heard music coming from downstairs, and it was the same song over and over again. It was Donnie McClurkin's "That's what I believe." After about the fifth time of hearing the same song, I cried one last time. I got up and went downstairs.

My aunt fixed me something to eat and I felt like something had been lifted off me. I didn't know what but something had. I showered, got dressed, and called Jazmyn. She was off so I headed over to see her. For the last three days, we had not talked as much as we usually did, and I missed her.

I got there and she opened the door. She was wearing her gown that had the snaps in the front. I laughed and said, "How old, are you? Eighty?" She laughed and told me that I should not talk about her gown.

We sat and talked; she asked how I really was doing and I told her that honestly, I was fine but I knew that this was coming. I told her that she was the first person I wanted to see but I had to grab a few things I left at the house and I would be back later. After a couple of hours, I got up to go. I gave her a hug. I went to leave but she held on to my hand and said, "I don't want you to leave." I asked her why as I pulled her back into me. She said, "Because I don't" and we kissed. And in this moment, I was so thankful for her snappy gown. Afterwards, I left and told her that I would be back.

When I got to my place, Janice had already been drinking. I headed to the basement to grab some stuff. She said, "You're really not coming back?" I told her no. She asked me if we could just please try to work things out. I told her no and especially not while she was still drinking. As I left, she called me stupid and yelled, "You know she's never going to be with you!" I shut the door and left. Ugh.

I hung with my aunt for a little before I went back out to Jazmyn's. In her drunken state Janice was blowing my phone up and leaving voicemails. In some of the messages she was telling me that she loved me; in some she was telling me that she hated me. I called her daughter and asked her to check on her mom and to make sure her sisters were ok. This continued for about three weeks, after which she called again. This time she was sober. She told me that she had started counseling and invited me to the next session. I agreed to go because you have to understand we were together for almost five years. I still loved her and wanted the best for her.

We went to counseling and the counselor had me listen to Janice's expressions of herself. She asked if I understood how Janice felt. She did not really allow me to express myself. So, I just sat there and listened to the session until I was dismissed. This seemed like a waste of money but if it was helping Janice, I guessed I would support it.

The next few weeks were like an up and down rollercoaster. I would spend time with Jazmyn but I had so many loose ends with Janice. We had a place together, plus all our other stuff. We had to split all the bills in our names. It was a mess.

Janice invited me over one afternoon so I went. When I got there, she had cooked all my favorite food. Cooking was something nobody could take away from her. The woman could cook! I ate as she talked to me, then she turned on some music and started dancing and one thing led to another, and I don't even have to say what happened next.

I felt terrible afterwards. Terrible like I cheated on Jazmyn even though we were technically not together, and terrible because I felt like I had just given Janice hope that we would be getting back together. I didn't know what had happened to me; I had gone from someone who used to not care about anything to constantly feeling torn. I did not like this person. This person felt weak, this person felt way too vulnerable, this person did not feel like me. Janice asked if I would consider coming back home and working things out and I told her the truth. I said No. She threw $300 at me and told me it was for the sex and that I should think about going into business. I picked up my stuff and left thinking, *Damn.*

Since I met Jazmyn it was like I couldn't lie. I couldn't even sugar-coat stuff to make it seem not as bad. This was the reason why even though it seemed harsh I had to tell Janice the truth when she asked if I was in love with someone else. It was like my player switch got turned off. Not only did it get turned off; it was like somebody ripped the cover off the wall and tore the wires out of the socket. What was happening to me?

CHAPTER 40

I went home and showered and then went over to Jazmyn's house. When I got there, we sat on her bed. I knew I had to tell her what happened, even if she decided she didn't want anything else to do with me; I couldn't keep anything from her. So, I told her every last humiliating detail and she just sat there and listened. She showed no facial expression change or anything. She just sat there and waited for me to finish and when I did, she wrapped her arms around me and said, "I can't be mad at you. I know how many feelings are still there." She then laughed and said, "But don't let it happen again." I told her I wouldn't and lay back and closed my eyes.

I told Janice she could have everything. I just wanted my stuff out of the basement, including my books and DVDs. There was only a year left on my SUV so she told me to keep it and continue making the payments.

I continued to work and spend time with Jazmyn. I just seemed to be in a different mind space; nothing really bothered me. It was easy to let things go. I have not said much about all the anger and rage I had inside of me because I really don't like to think about it.

I became an entirely different person when I got angry. I would get so mad that I would punch holes in walls or punch glass pictures and just sit there and watch my hand bleed. I can't tell you how many of my huge Scarface pictures I had hanging in my basement that I had to reframe. I sprained or caused damage to my hand several times from hitting beams in the wall. And it wasn't one particular thing that would set me off. It could be anything, and I would lose it and go from zero to ten and everything would go red. I chose to hit walls instead of people because I used to feel like if I actually hit a person, I wouldn't be able to stop myself. I would get so mad that I wanted to kill people and when I got like that there was nothing or nobody that could calm me down. Janice also had to put up with this when I would have my blackout drunk nights. Anyway, I just felt like all that anger disappeared and left my body. Jazmyn brought out a certain calmness in me; she brought balance to my life.

It wasn't long before Janice started using my car as a pawn and as much as I loved it, like everything else, I had to let it go. That was the only thing tying us together so my aunt followed me and I drove to Janice's place, parked it, and left the keys in the cup holder and bounced. I thought I would be more emotional about it but I wasn't. I had literally given up everything I thought I ever wanted and somehow, I was at peace with it.

A few months went by and Jazmyn and I decided to actually start dating. I had never been happier in my life. I agreed to go to church with her sometimes. I was starting to get a little interested in the Word but I really only went because it made her happy. Whatever I heard preached, I went and looked it up and started reading for myself.

I also started listening to Louis Farrakhan and looking into Islam. I started studying Egyptology. I read a book called *Thinking and Destiny* and started looking into Catholicism. I read the *Secret and the Power* and Eckhart Tolle's *New Earth*. I looked into the Metu Neter and New Age teachings. I started doing meditation listening to Deepak Chopra. I was on a search for the truth and I was reading anything I could to try to find it. And right as I was getting ready to order the Egyptian Book of the Dead something stopped me.

One day at church while the choir was singing and everybody was singing and clapping along, this little old black lady walked over to me and grabbed my hand and looked me in the eyes. You know, kind of how you see Cicely Tyson impart wisdom into somebody in a movie. She said, "God wants you to know he has a plan for you." And she smiled and walked away. I was just standing there like, "What?" Now I had a pretty good church people bull crap meter and not one red flag went off when this lady was talking. She didn't know me, I didn't know her, and the feeling I got was not like she was speaking to me but someone was speaking through her.

A few weeks later I was sitting in church and the preacher started preaching on God's forgiveness: "If we confess our sins, He is faithful and just to forgive sins and to cleanse us from all unrighteousness" (1 John 1:9). He went on to say that there was nothing that we could do that God wouldn't forgive. I kept thinking to myself, *Nothing? You mean nothing? All the things I did, all the hell that I raised, and it all can be wiped clean; it all can be forgiven?*

I was wrestling with this thought in my mind. It just didn't make sense. How could I have not heard this until now? Where was this message growing up? This couldn't be right! As Jazmyn's and my relationship grew, we continued to go to church. I didn't go to every service like her. She grew up in church and she would go every day if it was open. But I tried to go often. We were inseparable; we went everywhere together. And just when I thought nothing could come between us, it did.

Six months into the relationship Jazmyn came home and said, "We can't do this anymore; it's wrong." And I just sat there staring at her in disbelief. My mind couldn't even register what was happening.

"What do you mean we can't do this?" So, do you remember earlier when I told you who she belonged to?

She said, "It's wrong in the eyes of God and I've been struggling with it, and I love you, but I know this isn't right."

And Janice's words hit me like a ton of bricks. "She's never going to be with you." And I felt every single piece of the heart that I didn't even know I had shatter into a million pieces. I started crying and asked her, "Why didn't you just leave me where I was? What was the purpose of all this?"

She started crying and said that she knew we were supposed to be in each other's lives for a reason but not like this. She went on to tell me how sorry she was and how she allowed the enemy to pervert what God was trying to do with us. I looked at her like she was crazy. I was so furious and broken that my physical body couldn't express what my emotions were feeling, so I started sobbing. She kissed me and kissed me until I stopped crying and the very thing, she said we had to stop happened.

This continued for months, this up and down rollercoaster of we can't do this even though we were doing it, and the parts of me that loved her more than anything teetered between love and hate. Hate that she did this to me, hate that she did this to us. I was fine with her and her God when we were just friends. I would have never crossed that line without her permission. I hated everything including God. I wanted nothing to do with God anymore. What kind of sick torture was this? That rage that was gone was back and I had no way to release it.

CHAPTER 41

When I tried to talk to my friends back home no one believed that we weren't together, so they would just laugh and joke and I would just say to forget it. My family didn't seem to comprehend anything I was saying and I was left with only her (Jazmyn) to talk to, the source of my pain. How do you talk to the source about itself? So, I kept everything inside and I started drinking again to numb the pain.

At this time, I was working in the adult correction system and I hated it. The other C.O.s were worse than the inmates. I worked where there was a good old boys' club, a bunch of racist degenerates. Most of them should have been locked up themselves for the way they treated the inmates. I absolutely hated it. Some nights I would come home and have so much frustration about everything going on that I would just cry.

Everybody in the outside world thought I was ok; I was so used to wearing that mask that it was easy to pick it up and put it back on. I no longer wanted to be here. I didn't see the point. I constantly thought about dying and the only thing that was stopping me was that my baby brother was still in high school. I couldn't bear the thought of him having to bury his sister before he really began his life. Other than that, I knew everybody else would eventually be ok. Smiling and talking to people was becoming unbearable, but I kept up the facade because I couldn't let people know that the once-strong Jamihla couldn't even stand the thought of being here anymore. I had never been in this kind of darkness in my life and honestly had no idea how I was going to find my way out.

The correction facility I worked at was in my hometown but I still lived almost an hour and a half away. One night I was getting off and one of my friends invited me to come by. They said there would be some people there and they were kicking it. *Why not?* I thought. I had not kicked it in forever; it seemed like years. I would have one drink and head home. So, I got there and one beer turned into two. Jazmyn and I were messaging and she told me to stay there since I was drinking. That pissed me off because I was teetering on hate that day. I started saying stuff like, "Why, do you have somebody there?" And in my heart of hearts I knew it was my anger talking because she was not even that type of girl. But I told you once I hit that point there's no coming back.

One of my friends took my keys and hid them because she didn't want me driving. So I just lay down and played it cool until she went to sleep. I found my keys, took another drink, and I was off. I was on the highway, starting my hour and a half journey.

Jamihla had left the building and whatever it was that took over when I was angry and drunk was in full control. I had a whole other six pack of beer on the passenger seat. I was about twenty minutes into my drive when I started having thoughts that I should just end it, so I sped up. I was tired of everything, I was tired of everybody, I was tired of being here.

I called Jazmyn and we were arguing. She could tell that I was drinking. She was yelling at me, asking why I was driving when I had been drinking. And I was yelling back at her and I didn't even know why. This was how I got when hatred took over. I started driving faster. Something in my head was just yelling at me, "LET GO, LET GO, LET GO, LET GO. It could all be over if you just LET GO." Jazmyn was still talking in my ear and I thought to myself, *F*** it*. I let go and the voices stopped. And so did everything else.

I don't know how long I was out before I came around. It took me a minute to register where I was. I blinked and I saw blood. My eyes focused and there was blood everywhere. I was able to open the car door and get out. I looked up at the sky and yelled, "WHY, WHY AM I STILL HERE?" I was on the ground crying, "What do you want from me? Why won't you just let me go?"

Not only was I still here, I saw the flashing lights coming down the highway. Screw my life! I didn't want to go in the ambulance but it was either that or with the state trooper. I went to the hospital to get checked out. There were no major injuries: raccoon eyes from the impact and a little defect inside my nose that no one could see.

The trooper was trying to do a field sobriety test while I was in the hospital bed and I got super annoyed. My mother was there and she was upset, but I didn't know if it was because of the accident or how I was acting in the hospital. Jazmyn was also there and she was pissed. Oh, how much easier it would have been to just die.

I was charged with a DUI (driving under the influence), having an open container, and failure to control a vehicle. I didn't tell them why I actually wrecked; I told them a semi swerved in my lane and I overcorrected and hit the median. Jazmyn couldn't even be happy I was alive because she was so pissed that she had to live through thinking I was dead.

Not only did I fail at leaving this place, I had more problems than I started out with and I couldn't figure out why I was still here, why I kept being spared. I had to pay over $1,000 for an attorney, plus all my fines and court costs, only to have to go to jail anyway, go to AA meetings, and be placed on probation for two years.

After all my court matters were over, I went to work and I was called into the warden's office. He told me that I was fired because of the DUI. Technically, he did not have to terminate me but he did. So yeah, that was that! And did I mention my car was totaled?

I had just gotten a new car. They ended up having to pay me unemployment but still, how long would that last? My life was such a disaster I didn't know how things could get any worse.

EPILOGUE

I lay in bed thinking what a colossal screw-up I was, having no idea what I was going to do next. I heard this small, still voice and it said, "I WILL lay you down before I let you go back to your old life." As sure as my name is Jamihla, I was sure I knew who was speaking to me. It wasn't like that voice that taunted me for years about where I was going. It wasn't like the voice that told me to let go. It wasn't the voice that made me feel good about myself and inflated my ego when I had nothing to be proud about. It was the voice of a father; it was the voice of "The Father," and I was absolutely terrified.

This was a voice I had never heard before but it seemed more familiar than any other voice I had heard. And He was telling me if I went it was on His terms not mine, and before He would let me go back to where He had pulled me out of, He would pick the terms that He would take me out with, not me. Can you imagine hearing the voice of the Almighty God, the great I AM and it was as clear as the voice in your head reading this book, telling you that you did not get to decide what happens to you, He and only He would decide that?

"You will not go back to the life I've pulled you away from!" I still had free will but I knew full well the consequences of going backwards. The wages of sin is death and He was telling me He would decide the payment. I felt something else broke off me, like I did at my aunt's house when I couldn't move and she kept playing "That's what I believe" over and over again.

I picked up my Bible and started reading and over time God

began to show me who He really was. He was a father to the father-less, a healer to the broken, strength to the weak. He was there with me when I was hurting, He saw everything that happened. He saw how He was misrepresented; He saw the doors that others opened that unleashed demons in my life. He saw all of my struggles; He saw all of my pain.

He saw me being reckless; His heart broke knowing I thought I belonged to the enemy. He was bigger than any devil in hell.

"When they tried to take you out when you hit that pole, I cradled you and placed you in the only safe space left in that car. When that bullet almost hit you, it was I that blocked it. I saw them telling you to let go; it was I that formed a hedge of protection around you so you could walk out of that car. Your time is not up; you were saved for such a time as this. You want to know why you were spared: you were spared to tell your story so that somebody might live. Your story will be life to someone in a dead place. Your story will set captives free. Your story will show that no matter how hot the furnace gets; I will be standing in the midst and will pull you out. Hell dispatched its demons when you were a child to stop you from getting here. You have battled incest, rape, ridicule, homosex-uality, drug and alcohol abuse, depression, suicide, people constantly calling you what you are not. But you are who I say you are, and you have been called to set the captives free!"

The next Sunday that Jazmyn went to church I went with her. There was an altar call and something started pulling me; my feet were moving before my mind could even register what was happen-ing. In a sea of people, I felt like He was talking directly to me and only me. And in that moment, I asked God to forgive me for all my sin and to come into my heart.

Shortly after, on July 3, 2013, I was baptized and completely committed to God. The devil no longer had a hold on me and my life would never be the same. It would be a lie to tell you that my life became easy and it was smooth sailing once I accepted Jesus as my Lord and Savior.

There were seventeen years' worth of sin and bondage that had to be broken off me, and it was a process. But it was all worth it knowing that somebody might live; it was all worth it knowing that I was no longer damned, knowing that I was free.

Jazmyn and I ended up completely separating and living in separate places. There was a lot of healing that needed to take place but through time, God slowly but surely repaired those broken places and brought us back together, and our friendship was even stronger than it was before.

I went on to become a Paramedic and I love what I do. I was a part of an organization that helps people struggling with addiction through the word of our testimony. I also started a mentoring group for young girls with my best friend Monique called Daddy's Little Girl's to empower and encourage young girls to become everything God has called them to be. One of the greatest experiences I've had besides seeing some of my family members and friends give their life to Christ was when I was in the back of the ambulance with an eighty-year-old lady who had been hurt in church when she was a small child and never went back. She said she always wanted to know God and every time she went to church; she was made to feel ashamed and embarrassed so she just stopped going. She was up in age now and could no longer see to try to read the Bible, and she could no longer hear well enough to listen to it.

Our entire conversation revolved around me holding her hand and speaking directly into her ear. I told her of my experience with church and that I now knew God and I asked her if she would like to invite Him in. She gave her life to Christ right there in the back of that ambulance and said she felt like her life had changed in that one ambulance ride. And at that moment I knew how true God's words were when he said, "You were sent to set the captives free!"

PRAYER OF SALVATION

If you have been touched by this book, *Broken Road to Redemption*, and are ready to surrender your life to Jesus, pray this prayer with me:

God, I thank you for loving me so much that You sent Your Son Jesus to die on the cross for my sins. Jesus, I am a sinner in need of a Savior. I ask You to forgive me. I surrender all to you. I cannot do it on my own. I ask You, Jesus, to come into my life. I give You control and I ask that You will rule and reign in my heart so that Your will would be accomplished in my life. Holy Spirit fill me, comfort me and guide me. I am Yours in Jesus' name.

Satan, I renounce you. You are no longer lord of my life. Blood of Jesus, break every curse of sin, every evil spirit attacking my life, every mind battle. I take authority in Jesus name. The hold you had over my life is broken in the name of Jesus. Thank You, Jesus, Amen!

If you are depressed, have had thoughts of harming yourself or are battling addiction please don't be ashamed or afraid to seek help. Below are some resources for anyone struggling with the things listed above.

National Suicide Prevention Lifeline
1-800-273-8255

SAMHSA's Nation Helpline
(Substance Abuse and Mental Health Services Administration)
1-800-662-HELP (4357)